Comptroller of the Currency
Administrator of National Banks

I0448321

Custody Services

Comptroller's Handbook

January 2002.

Asset Management

Custody Services   Table of Contents

Custody Services   Overview

Background

This booklet addresses the fundamentals of securities custody and related services, and provides guidance for examining those activities in national banks. One of a series of specialized asset management booklets in the *Comptroller's Handbook*, the booklet supplements the overall guidance in the "Asset Management Supervision" booklet as well as the "Large Bank Supervision" and "Community Bank Fiduciary Activities" booklets. For additional guidance on general asset management operations and controls, please refer to *the Comptroller's Handbook for Asset Management*. Please refer to this booklet's glossary for definitions of terms used in this handbook.

The Custody Services Industry

The ability to gather assets, effectively employ technology, and efficiently process huge volumes of transactions is essential in the custody business today. With the growth of the investment industry during the past two decades, particularly in the mutual fund arena, the level of assets under custody has increased significantly. Competition for custody of those assets has been fierce, causing profit margins to shrink. At the same time, the industry has focused on using technology to improve efficiency. As a result, a handful of large banks now dominate the custody services industry.

Services Provided by a Custodian

Services provided by a bank custodian are typically the settlement, safekeeping, and reporting of customers' marketable securities and cash. A custody relationship is contractual, and services performed for a customer may vary. Banks provide custody services to a variety of customers, including mutual funds and investment managers, retirement plans, bank fiduciary and agency accounts, bank marketable securities accounts, insurance companies, corporations, endowments and foundations, and private banking clients. Banks that are not major custodians may provide custody services for their customers through an arrangement with a large custodian bank.

Core Custody Services

A custodian providing core domestic custody services typically settles trades, invests cash balances as directed, collects income, processes corporate actions, prices securities positions, and provides recordkeeping and reporting services.

Global Custody Services

A global custodian provides custody services for cross-border securities transactions. In addition to providing core custody services in a number of foreign markets, a global custodian typically provides services such as executing foreign exchange transactions and processing tax reclaims. A global custodian typically has a sub-custodian, or agent bank, in each local market to help provide custody services in the foreign country. The volume of global assets under custody has grown rapidly in recent years as investors have looked to foreign countries for additional investment opportunities.

Securities Lending and Other Value-Added Services

A bank may offer securities lending to its custody customers. Securities lending can allow a customer to make additional income on its custody assets by loaning its securities to approved borrowers on a short-term basis. In addition, a custodian may contract to provide its customers with other value-added services such as performance measurement, risk measurement, and compliance monitoring.

Risks Associated with Custody Services

For purposes of the OCC's discussion of risk, the OCC assesses banking risk relative to its impact on capital and earnings. From a supervisory perspective, risk is the potential that events, expected or unexpected, may have an adverse impact on a bank's capital or earnings. The OCC has defined nine categories of risk for bank supervision purposes: credit, interest rate, liquidity, price, foreign currency translation, transaction, compliance, strategic, and reputation. These categories are not mutually exclusive; any product or service may expose a bank to multiple risks. For analysis and discussion, however, the OCC identifies and assesses the risks separately. The primary risks associated with custody services are: transaction, compliance, credit, strategic, and reputation. These risks are discussed more fully in the following paragraphs.

Transaction Risk

Transaction risk is the current and prospective risk to earnings or capital from fraud, error, and the inability to deliver products or services, maintain a competitive position, and manage information. Risk is inherent in efforts to gain strategic advantage, and in the failure to keep pace with changes in the financial services marketplace. **Transaction risk is evident in each product and service offered.** Transaction risk encompasses product development and delivery, transaction processing, systems development, computing systems, the complexity of products and services, and the internal control environment.

Transaction risk is also referred to as operational risk. This risk is inherently high in custody services because of the high volume of transactions processed daily. Experience in the custody field has shown that errors in corporate action, settlement, foreign exchange (FX), and operating (suspense) account processing are common causes of losses attributable to custody activities. These losses, individually and in the aggregate, may be material. Effective risk identification and control can greatly mitigate these errors.

Effective policies and procedures, a strong control environment, and efficient use of technology are essential risk management tools. Meaningful reporting, based on accurate and reliable data, is needed to provide management with monitoring tools. The risks may be magnified in a global custody operation where transactions occur around the clock in a variety of different markets. A global custodian must consider a variety of additional factors including differing market rules and conventions, the degree of automation in the foreign market, different types of securities, capital or currency restrictions, and the availability and communication of timely and accurate information.

Compliance Risk

Compliance risk is the current and prospective risk to earnings or capital arising from violations of, or nonconformance with, laws, rules, regulations, prescribed practices, internal policies and procedures, or ethical standards. Compliance risk also arises in situations where the laws or rules governing certain bank products or activities of a bank's clients may be ambiguous or untested. Compliance risk exposes the institution to fines, civil money penalties, payment of damages, and the voiding of contracts. Compliance risk can also lead to a diminished reputation, reduced franchise value, limited business opportunities, reduced expansion potential, and an inability to enforce contracts.

Custody services are contractual in nature, and a bank must ensure compliance with the provisions of all applicable agreements. A strong compliance program should include monitoring the variety of laws and regulations that may affect a custodian's business and reporting any material changes to the customer. Global custodians in particular must be aware of the regulatory environments in which they operate. Compliance risk may be heightened in foreign markets because different markets have different rules and regulations. These differences make supervision challenging.

Credit Risk

Credit risk is the current and prospective risk to earnings or capital arising from an obligor's failure to meet the terms of any contract with the bank or otherwise to perform as agreed. Credit risk is found in all activities that depend on counterparty, issuer, or borrower performance. It arises any time funds are extended, committed, invested, or otherwise exposed through actual or implied contractual agreements, whether reflected on or off the balance sheet.

The U.S. market settlement practice of delivery versus payment (DVP) virtually eliminates counterparty credit risk in the settlement process. However, a custodian may be exposed to credit risk if it advances funds to settle trades for a customer. In addition, securities lending activities may expose a bank to counterparty credit risk. For further information on credit risk please refer to the *Comptroller's Handbook*.

Global custodians may be exposed to credit risk from several sources. First, if a sub-custodian fails, the custodian may have difficulty obtaining its customers' securities. Second, not all markets settle transactions DVP, so there is risk if the custodian delivers securities without receiving payment or pays without receiving securities. Third, in some markets a custodian may offer contractual settlement. In this case, a custodian makes the entries to its customer's account on the contractual settlement date even if the custodian hasn't actually received the cash or securities needed to settle the trade. Here, the credit risk is with the global custodian's customer. Contract provisions should provide for reversal of the transaction if the trade fails or a specified amount of time passes.

Strategic Risk

Strategic risk is the current and prospective risk to earnings or capital arising from adverse business decisions, improper implementation of decisions, or lack of responsiveness to industry changes. This risk depends on the compatibility of an organization's strategic goals, the business strategies developed to achieve those goals, the resources deployed toward these goals, and the quality of implementation. The resources needed to carry out business strategies are both tangible and intangible. They include communication channels, operating systems, delivery networks, and managerial capacities and capabilities. The organization's internal characteristics must be evaluated against the impact of economic, technological, competitive, regulatory, and other environmental changes.

A bank's decision to participate in the custody business, and its ability to be competitive if it does, is a source of strategic risk to the bank. The industry has seen increased competition in recent years, which has reduced margins and forced industry consolidation. To compete, a custodian must be able to achieve a size that creates an economy of scale, and continually invest in systems and technology.

Reputation Risk

Reputation risk is the current and prospective impact on earnings and capital arising from negative public opinion. This affects the institution's ability to establish new relationships or services or to continue servicing existing relationships. This risk may expose the institution to litigation, financial loss, or a decline in its customer base. Reputation risk exposure is present throughout the organization and includes the responsibility to exercise an abundance of caution in dealing with its customers and community.

The importance of a custodian's reputation cannot be overstated. The ability of the bank to deliver services as promised is critical to maintaining its reputation. The transaction-oriented custody services business makes a bank's failure to perform a contracted service highly visible to its customer. Virtually any problem that the bank encounters in its custody business line can affect its reputation if it is made public.

A bank's custody customers may also be exposed to interest rate, liquidity, price, credit, and foreign currency translation risk through the assets they hold in their custody accounts. Although any related losses are not direct risks to the bank providing custody services, some customers may hold the bank at fault for them. The possibility that these customers will make their claims or allegations public presents some reputation risk.

Risk Management

Examiners should determine whether a bank has adequate systems in place to identify, measure, monitor, and control risks in the custody services area. Such systems include policies, procedures, internal controls, and management information systems governing custody services.

Effective internal control is essential to a bank's management of the risks found in custody services. A properly designed and consistently enforced system of internal controls will help management safeguard assets under custody, produce reliable financial reports, and comply with laws and regulations. For additional discussion of the internal control environment, refer to the "Internal Control" booklet of the *Comptroller's Handbook*.

Operational Controls

The importance of operational controls in the custody services area cannot be overemphasized. Custody is a volume-driven, transaction-processing business, and much of the risk associated with it is operational in nature. For this reason, strong operational controls are essential to effectively manage transaction risk.

Separation of Duties
Control can best be achieved through a division of duties. A bank first segregates administrative and operational functions, and then it segregates duties (both physical and logical access) within the operating system itself. It is the responsibility of management to assess the control environment and ensure that an appropriate system of internal control, including separation of duties, is in place.

Dual Control
Assets under custody should be properly controlled and safeguarded at all times. Dual control procedures should ensure that one person, acting alone, does not have the ability to complete all phases of a transaction, or move custody assets. Procedures should require dual control in processing of all

custody assets, including securities, cash, income payments, and corporate actions.

Accounting Controls

Independent control processes should ensure the accuracy of a custodian's records and accounting systems. Accounting controls are used to monitor and measure transactional work flows and their accuracy. Accounting controls include blotters, reconcilement of cash and asset movements, and suspense accounts.

Account Acceptance and Monitoring

The account acceptance process is the first step in risk management. The risks associated with an individual account should be addressed prior to acceptance. A custodian's acceptance process should provide an adequate review of the customer's needs and wants. During the acceptance process, the custodian should also assess whether its duties are within its capabilities, are lawful, and can be performed profitably.

Procedures

A properly documented account acceptance process will provide sufficient information for the bank to make an informed decision. Risk-based procedures should provide sales personnel with "front-end guidance" related to the review and acceptance of new accounts, and should include a bank's requirements related to customer due diligence and required documentation.

Assessment of New Business

The due diligence process should ensure that the services the customer wants the custodian to perform are legal (in the relevant jurisdictions) and within the custodian's capabilities. The account acceptance process should include an assessment of the proposed relationship including a review of the products and services needed by the customer, likely transactions (type and volume), and customer information necessary to facilitate custody transactions (such as tax information related to foreign tax relief). The due diligence process should include a review for compliance with anti-money laundering rules. Please refer to the "Bank Secrecy Act/Anti-Money Laundering" booklet of the *Comptroller's Handbook* for further information.

When accepting new business the bank should consider the operational needs of the account. The bank should consult all applicable departments (including legal, accounting, operations, credit, and compliance) to determine whether it has the capacity to serve the customer without incurring unreasonable costs.

Agreements
Custody relationships are contractual in nature and are essentially directed agencies. The customer is the principal, and the custodian is the agent. The custody agreement is important as a risk management tool. The agreement should clearly establish the custodian's duties and responsibilities. Custody agreements should be standardized when possible, and any deviations from the standardized agreement should be reviewed prior to acceptance.

Management Information Systems

A management information system (MIS) is a system or process that provides the information necessary to manage an organization effectively. MIS and the information it generates are generally considered essential to internal control. A primary objective of custody services MIS is the management of transaction risk. Sound MIS produces information that is accurate, timely, consistent, complete, and relevant. It allows a bank to measure operational performance to designated benchmarks. While a custodian's MIS enables a bank to determine whether its operations are profitable, it should also inform management about other essential matters, such as whether internal controls are working. Refer to the "Management Information System" booklet of the *Comptroller's Handbook* for additional information.

Contingency Plan
A contingency plan is an extension of a bank's system of internal control and physical security. The plans should include provisions for continuance of operation, and recovery when threats may damage or disrupt the institution's data processing support. A bank that relies on an outside servicer for the bulk of its data processing should take steps to determine whether the contingency plans of the servicer are adequate and whether its own plans complement those of the servicer.

Comprehensive contingency planning policies and procedures for all business lines are a responsibility of the board of directors and senior management of a national bank. The board is responsible for reviewing and approving the institution's contingency plans annually and documenting the reviews in its minutes.

Board and Management Supervision

National bank directors are expected to perform general supervision over a bank's activities. Directors may assign the administration of custody activities to such officers, directors, employees, or committees as they may designate. However, directors retain the overall responsibility for supervision. Any workable system or organization of a custody operation may be acceptable as long as the directors are fully aware of and are fulfilling their responsibilities.

Staffing

Capable management and appropriate staffing are essential to effective risk management. Experienced staff, adequate training, and the ability to manage turnover play a major role in a bank's ability to offer high quality and consistent performance in custody services. A bank must carefully compare its custody staffing levels with the volume of business and the complexity of the services offered. If staffing is not adequate to handle the volume of business, transactions may be poorly executed, customer service may be inadequate, and the bank may lose both dollars and customers.

Compliance

The board and management are responsible for ensuring that a bank's custody activities comply with applicable laws and regulations. All applicable laws and regulations relevant to the custody business should be identified and communicated to the appropriate personnel. The custodian should have a system in place to monitor for compliance with applicable laws and regulations.

Some of the compliance issues that may arise for custodians are compliance with local law, recordkeeping and confirmation requirements, shareholder communication, mutual fund custody, retirement plan assets, fiduciary activities, anti-money laundering, securities lending, and free-riding.

Local Law
Custodians, particularly global custodians, may be affected by a variety of laws and regulations. In addition to U.S. federal laws and regulations, the custodian may be subject to state laws, and laws of foreign countries in which they offer services. In foreign countries, the global custodian will typically

rely on its sub-custodian to understand and comply with local laws and regulations. Local laws may address such issues as:

- *Fiduciary capacity.* A custodian may be considered to be a fiduciary under law in some jurisdictions.
- *Unclaimed property.* Most states have an unclaimed property law. These provisions may require a custodian to escheat unclaimed property to the state. ERISA preempts state unclaimed property laws for retirement plan assets. Globally, unclaimed property laws vary widely.
- *Taxation.* Countries' tax policies on investment income and capital gains differ. The United States may have tax treaties with other countries that provide tax relief.
- *Money laundering or suspicious activity.* To prevent money laundering and other illegal activities, a wide range of laws and regulations exist that may require banks to identify customers and report suspicious activities.
- *Reporting and recordkeeping.* A custodian may be subject to regulatory reporting and recordkeeping requirements in the countries in which it offers services.

Global custodians operate in multiple regulatory environments. They must have an effective process in place to identify regulatory and market changes and ensure continued compliance.

Securities Transactions
12 CFR 12 establishes minimum recordkeeping and confirmation requirements for securities transactions handled by national banks. The regulation also requires that banks establish policies and procedures covering supervision of securities transactions and reporting of personal transactions.

Shareholder Communications
The Shareholder Communications Act and implementing SEC regulations address banks' proxy processing. The objective of these rules is to ensure that beneficial owners of securities are provided proxy material and other corporate communications in a timely manner.

Mutual Funds
The Investment Company Act of 1940 and 17 CFR 240.17f address the custody of investment company (mutual fund) assets. In 2000, the SEC revised rule 17f-5, which addresses custody of fund assets outside the United States, and added a rule 17f-7 to address custody of fund assets with foreign

securities depositories. For the complete text of the final rule, refer to appendix C.

Retirement Plan Assets

A bank providing custody for retirement plan assets may have additional duties under the Employee Retirement Income Security Act (ERISA). What follows are examples of ERISA's implications in the custody services area:

- The Department of Labor (DOL) approved a class exemption relating to foreign exchange transactions of employee benefit plans. Prohibited Transaction Exemption (PTE) 98-54 is a class exemption that permits certain foreign exchange transactions between employee benefit plans and certain banks and broker-dealers that are parties in interest with respect to such plans, pursuant to standing instructions from an independent fiduciary of the plan.
- In Harris Trust v. Salomon Smith Barney, 530 U.S. 238 (2000), the Supreme Court held that section 502(a)(3) authorizes a "participant, beneficiary, or fiduciary" of a plan to bring a civil action against a nonfiduciary "party in interest" to redress violations of ERISA. Refer to the Supreme Court decision for further information.
- The DOL also issued class exemptions relating to securities lending in ERISA accounts. See "Securities Lending" below.

Laws or regulations of other countries may also apply to the custodian or the sub-custodian when pension assets of another country are held in custody.

Fiduciary Activities

Custody is generally not considered a fiduciary capacity under 12 CFR 9. However, a custodian may perform functions that are fiduciary in nature. For example, a custodian exercising discretion in managing a securities lending cash collateral pool would be acting in a fiduciary capacity and must comply with the relevant provisions of 12 CFR 9.

Anti-Money Laundering Recordkeeping and Reporting

31 CFR 103 addresses bank recordkeeping and reporting requirements for certain financial transactions. Records are required to be maintained for many transaction types including wire transfers, deposit account activity, and certain extensions of credit. Reporting requirements include suspicious activities, currency transactions, and reports of foreign financial accounts. In addition, 12 CFR 21 requires that banks establish a program for monitoring

Bank Secrecy Act compliance. For additional information on Bank Secrecy Act and anti-money laundering compliance issues, refer to the "Bank Secrecy Act/Anti-Money Laundering" booklet of the *Comptroller's Handbook*.

Securities Lending

Securities lending activities of national banks are subject to the requirements of Banking Circular 196, "Securities Lending." This issuance establishes guidelines for securities lending programs, as endorsed by the FFIEC. Securities lending activities of national banks are addressed in the "Securities Lending" section of this booklet.

The Department of Labor approved a class exemption relating to securities lending transactions by employee benefit plans. Prohibited Transaction Exemption (PTE) 81-6 and 82-63 establish specific conditions, which if followed, create a class exemption that permits employee benefit plans to lend securities to banks and broker-dealers that are parties in interest with respect to such plans.

Free-Riding in Custody Accounts

Free-riding, also known as day-trading, is the practice of buying and selling securities, usually on the same day, with the intention of paying for the purchase from the proceeds of the sale. The person doing the trading sets up a custody account at a bank and advises the broker that payments for trades will be made through the custody account. The free-rider generally has little or no money at risk. If the money is not in the account when the securities are delivered in a DVP transaction, the bank that completes the transaction creates a temporary overdraft and an extension of credit that is subject to the margin requirements in Regulation U (12 CFR 221). Free-riding schemes frequently involve initial public offerings.

Banking Circular 275, "Free Riding in Custody Accounts," alerts national banks to potential free-riding problems and risks. Banks that permit free-riding risk violation of Regulation U, or aiding and abetting violations of Regulation X (12 CFR 224) or Regulation T (12 CFR 220), as well as assuming the risk that the funds advanced to settle a transaction may not be recoverable from the customer. Banks should ensure that procedures for accepting new accounts include an inquiry into transactions identified in Banking Circular 275. Credit lines should be considered for any account that engages in this activity.

Global Sub-Custodian Network

A global custodian's network of agent banks in the local markets is crucial to its ability to provide efficient securities settlement and asset servicing to its customers. These agent banks are known as sub-custodians. The global custodian relies on its sub-custodian network to provide it with valuable information on the local markets, including the securities settlement systems, market conventions, and the regulatory environment.

Due Diligence — Markets

Before a global custodian selects a sub-custodian for a particular country, the global custodian must decide whether it should offer custody services in that market. There are a wide variety of foreign markets ranging from the mature markets of Western Europe to the emerging markets of Eastern Europe and Africa. Realistically, the decision to enter a market is driven by the customer's desire to invest there; nevertheless, the global custodian should conduct a due diligence review prior to entry.

Factors that should be considered include:

- Country risk, including the political, social, and economic environment;
- Banking and securities markets, including the regulatory environment and quality of supervision, existence of insider trading/fraud rules and bankruptcy laws, and the enforceability of laws and regulations;
- The settlement environment, including the degree of automation, the central securities depository (CSD), payment systems, and the typical settlement period;
- Restrictions on foreign investment, including registration of foreign shares, ability to repatriate capital, exit taxes, and currency controls;
- Investability of the market, including liquidity and depth;
- Availability and integrity of financial information; and
- Ability to offer custody services profitably.

Due Diligence — Sub-Custodian banks

Once the decision is made to enter a market, the global custodian must select a sub-custodian. The sub-custodian may be a local branch or an affiliate of the global custodian, but more often it is a local bank. A bank or banking group may act as a "regional" custodian, providing local custody services in several countries within a geographical region (e.g., Eastern Europe). The board and management should ensure that an effective sub-custodian selection process is in place. Factors that should be considered include:

· A review of the institution's financial strength and insurance coverage;
· Position in the market and local market knowledge;
· Internal control environment, including policies and procedures, systems and controls in place to ensure accuracy of records, and the ability to keep assets safe;
· The likelihood of U.S. jurisdiction over and enforcement of judgments against a foreign sub-custodian;
· The degree of automation, and plans for future systems development;
· Quality and experience of personnel; and
· If assets held by the sub-custodian will include assets of a U.S. mutual fund, whether the sub-custodian meets the requirements of SEC Rule 17f.

When a sub-custodian has been selected, the parties should enter into a contract that sets out the duties and responsibilities of both parties. In addition, global custodians should continually monitor its sub-custodians. At a minimum, the sub-custodian's financial condition, performance, and internal controls should be monitored to ensure that it continues to meet the global custodian's requirements.

Safekeeping and Settlement

The custody business developed from safekeeping and settlement services provided to customers for a fee. Banks originally provided only basic safekeeping services for their customers. Although banks routinely settled trades and processed income for their own investments, their customers had to clip their own coupons, collect dividends, and take their securities out of safekeeping to settle trades or for bond maturities. Realizing that their expertise in securities processing and their image as a safe repository would be valuable to their customers, banks began to promote their securities processing ability.

The custody industry has grown to global proportions, but has maintained a low profile. Custodians have been instrumental in consolidating holdings and providing expertise for a wide variety of assets held by its customers. Global custodians control trillions of dollars in assets in offices around the world.

Safekeeping of Custody Assets

A custodial bank is responsible for maintaining the safety of custody assets held in physical form at one of the custodian's premises, a sub-custodian facility, or an outside depository. A custodian's accounting records and internal controls should ensure that assets of each custody account are kept separate from the assets of the custodian and maintained under joint control. National banks may hold assets off-premises if they maintain adequate safeguards and controls and if such care is consistent with applicable law.

On-Premises Custody
The G-30 marketplace settlement goal of T + 1 will make it virtually impossible for bank custodians to hold marketable securities in physical form. A custodian will not be able to remove a certificate from a vault and ensure delivery to the broker in time for settlement. However, non-depository-eligible securities and miscellaneous assets (e.g., jewelry, art, coins) must be kept in physical form by a custodian.

When a bank custodian holds assets in physical form in its vault, the bank should provide for security devices consistent with applicable law and sound custodial management. The custodian should have appropriate lighting, alarms, and other physical security controls. Vault control procedures should ensure segregation of custody assets from bank assets, dual control over custody assets, maintenance of records evidencing access to the vault, and proper asset transfers.

Assets should only be out of the vault when the custodian receives or delivers the assets following purchases, sales, deposits, distributions, corporate actions, or maturities. Securities movement and control records should detail all asset movements, deposits, and withdrawals, including temporary withdrawals. The vault record should include the initials of the joint custodians, the date of vault transactions, description and amounts of assets, identity of the affected accounts, and the reasons that assets are withdrawn. Some custodians monitor their physical vault asset movement by using a computerized securities movement and control (SMAC) system which records the actual location of off-premises assets and monitors the movement of an asset during purchase, sale, or lending.

Global custodians having offices in foreign countries or using sub-custodians should develop processes to ensure that the operations at those sites have proper internal controls to protect assets. Refer to the sub-custodian section of this booklet for more information.

Off-Premises Custody

Changes in the marketplace and the large volume of securities traded each day have permanently altered the landscape of the custody world. The vast majority of custodial assets are held in book entry form. The major depositories in the United States are the Federal Reserve (for government securities) and the Depository Trust and Clearing Corporation (DTCC) (for equity and debt securities other than U.S. government securities). Currently, Euroclear and Clearstream (formerly Cedel) are two major international depositories. Each country will have at least one CSD such as DTCC in the United States. Mergers and consolidations of depositories are occurring regularly to streamline global securities processing. Custodians must be ready to adapt to the rapid evolution of the securities processing world with sound internal controls to safeguard assets.

Bank custodians may participate directly with a depository, or they may "piggyback" by using a correspondent bank to provide custody services to their customers in a private label format. In either case, the custodian should use SAS 70 reports or third-party audits whenever possible to ensure that an adequate control environment exists and that the depository has established sound safeguards.

Custodians should establish strong risk-based internal controls to protect assets held off-premises. Internal controls may be either active or passive. Active controls require dual control over the authorization of all transaction information prior to data entry. Passive controls are detective or reactive in nature. Passive controls may include independent reconcilements, overdraft reports, and failed trade reports.

Custodians should reconcile changes in the depository's position each day that a change in the position occurs, as well as completing a full-position reconcilement at least monthly. Depository position changes are generally the results of trade settlements, free deliveries (assets transferred off the depository position when no cash is received), and free receipts (assets being deposited or transferred to the depository position for new accounts when no cash is paid out). When controls on free deliveries are passive, personnel independent of the free delivery and free receipt asset movement process should reconcile changes in daily positions. Independent personnel should reconcile the depository's position report to the custodian's accounting system each month. Exceptions noted in the control systems should be reported to management in a timely manner.

Electronic terminal interfaces used to effect depository withdrawals, affirm trades, and deliver instructions to a depository should be subject to appropriate access controls (ID and password) and periodic audits. Each person with electronic terminal interface access should have a separate ID and password and should be able to perform only functions necessary for their job. IDs should not be shared. The person (normally the system administrator) responsible for granting access to the system that interfaces with a depository should be independent of the securities processing activity.

Job profiles should be developed for each job or position that needs to use system functions. The profile should contain a detailed description of the job and the reason system access is needed. The profile description should also outline those functions and systems that must be considered incompatible responsibilities in order to keep duties properly separated. A security procedure in the system administration process should monitor ID changes and ID issuance to ensure that duties remain properly separated. Such a procedure ensures, for example, that a reconciler could not move assets from a depository and then certify that the system is in balance.

Settlement of Securities Transactions

The risks associated with securities settlement will only increase as the securities markets become truly global. New technologies allow for faster movement of money from market to market. New and different securities products are being developed that require custodians to know the basic investment characteristics of each type of security they handle. Managing the risk of global securities settlement is a key to successful custody operations for national banks.

Basics of Securities Settlement

The securities settlement process contains some element of risk at each stage of the transaction. A national bank must make sure that it effectively manages each process in the transaction: trade initiation, trade affirmation, trade settlement, and trade compliance. The bank should use rapid and accurate communication among all participants to reduce the likelihood of a failed trade or loss.

The trading environment and securities settlement cycles are constantly undergoing changes to reduce risk and take advantage of technological developments. Trade settlement standards are moving to T (same day trade) or T + 1 from the three-day (T + 3) settlement standard for U.S. equities. U.S. government securities and other U.S. domestic fixed income trades generally settle in a T or T + 1 trading cycle. The shortening of the settlement period reduces a counterparty's credit risk and market risk in price-sensitive securities.

Trade Initiation

Transactions to buy or sell securities are initiated in a variety of ways. Bank custody customers may deliver buy or sell instructions to the bank by phone or fax. Some customers may place trades with their broker and inform the custodian of the terms of the trade by phone, fax, or electronic terminal. In some cases the customer, usually through an investment advisor, will place the trade with the broker and affirm the trade with the depository. In this case the bank custodian will receive instructions for settlement of the trade from the depository or settling agent. A national bank should have a process in place to ensure that a customer's instructions are clear, arrive in an agreed-upon format, and are properly documented (by electronic instruction, recorded phone line, fax, or in writing). The date the trade is executed is known as the trade date, and is referred to as "T" or T + 0.

Trade Affirmation/Confirmation

The trade affirmation/confirmation process occurs when a depository forwards the selling broker's confirmation of the transaction to the buyer's custodian. The custodian reviews the trade instructions from the depository and matches the information to instructions for the trade received from its customer. If the instructions match, the custodian affirms the trade. If the instructions do not match, then the custodian will "DK" (don't know, or reject) the trade or will instruct the selling broker how to handle the mismatch. The affirmation/confirmation process is generally completed by T + 1 in a normal T + 3 settlement cycle. On day T + 2, depositories usually send settlement instructions to the custodian bank after affirmation and prior to settlement date. The instructions contain the details of the trade that has been affirmed and agreed to by the parties in the trade. Custodians will match the settlement instructions to their records and prepare instructions to their wire department to send funds or expect funds from the depository on T + 3 of the settlement cycle.

Trade Settlement

Trade settlement occurs when securities and money are moved to complete the trade. Settlement occurs on T + 3 in a T + 3 settlement cycle. The depository sends a settlement report to all participants on the activities for their account. The custodian should review and reconcile the depository's settlement report to its activity report each day that asset positions change at the depository. The custodian should also compare the cash movement activity in its deposit account with its daily cash accounting control records. National banks should have a process to reconcile the changes in the depository position each day and should perform a full position reconcilement at least monthly.

Trade Compliance

Trade compliance is the internal control process used by custodians to manage trade transactions. In this process, the custodian determines that the customer's account has the securities on hand to deliver for sales, that the customer's account has adequate cash or forecasted cash for purchases, that trades are properly matched or DK'd, and that the depository's settlement instructions agree with the custodian's SMAC system. A national bank using a properly executed trade compliance system may prevent failed trades and needless reversals of transactions.

A national bank's trade compliance system should be able to detect free-riding attempts. A bank that permits free-riding may violate Regulation U (12CFR 221), may aid and abet violations of Regulation X (12 CFR 224) or Regulation T (12 CFR 220), and may assume the risk that it will be unable to recover from the customer the funds advanced to settle a transaction.

The Future of Securities Settlement

The basics of settlement as previously outlined will have to change to meet industry needs and lower risk in the system. Banks lacking a forward-looking technology strategy may find themselves at a competitive disadvantage. National banks offering custody services should develop strategies that use new technology to address risk and the T + 1 or shorter settlement cycle.

Banks should assess their technological readiness now to maintain a competitive position. Straight-through processing (STP), electronic trade confirmation (ETC), and standing instruction databases (SID) are technological processes designed to facilitate the future of domestic and global securities settlement. The goal of STP and T+1 is to minimize operational risk in trade processing. Custodians that do not develop technology strategies for custody services may be faced with trying to outsource trade settlement operations.

International Trade Settlement

The same basic settlement process applies whether the transaction is domestic or international. However, each foreign market has different exchanges, regulations, and settlement conventions. These differences present risks that national bank custodians must consider and address. It is essential that a sub-custodian has in-depth market knowledge. Additional issues that must be considered when trading international securities include:

- Legal and regulatory framework.
- Currency or capital controls.
- Registration of securities.[1]
- In-country processing (trading and custody) requirements.
- Local market conventions, such as:
  - Settlement cycle.
  - Use of central securities depository.
  - Availability of DVP in the market.
  - Methods of payment (real-time gross settlement, net settlement, central bank accounts, checks).
  - Degree of automation.
  - Trade execution.
  - Trade affirmation/confirmation process.
  - Delivery and safekeeping of securities (physical vs. book-entry).
- Different currencies used for settlement.
- Whether the custodian offers contractual settlement.
- Taxation.
- Local reporting obligations.

National banks should have a process in place to identify applicable laws and monitor compliance with laws of the countries in which they may be settling

---

[1] Many countries limit by percent the foreign ownership of their domestic securities. This creates a "dual" local and foreign market, which may cause problems by delaying registration of the beneficial ownership. The result may be a price difference between foreign and local shares. Issues may arise related to lost income, corporate actions, securities sales, and securities lending.

transactions. Bank custodians should attempt to use depositories and sub-custodians that provide DVP settlement for all cross-border trades.

A national bank may choose to provide contractual settlement to its customers in some markets as a competitive strategy. In contractual settlement, the customer is credited with the sale proceeds on the contractual settlement date regardless of whether the proceeds have been received. Conversely, even if purchased securities are not received, the customer's account is debited on the contractual settlement date. The bank should manage the risk of offering contractual settlement by incorporating in the agreement an understanding that if a transaction does not settle in an agreed-upon time, the transaction will be reversed.

Reporting and Recordkeeping

An important part of any custodian's business strategy is to provide its customers with recordkeeping and reporting services. The recordkeeping services should meet the customers' specialized needs and comply with applicable recordkeeping and reporting laws and regulations. Custodians should be able to generate customized customer reports as well as required regulatory and legal reports.

Custody customers have different reporting needs ranging from only quarterly reports to real-time on-line access. Some customers, especially those involved in mutual fund management, may need customized daily reports of their activity in domestic stocks and bonds, foreign securities, derivatives, options, or other unusual investments. Customers may also require multicurrency recordkeeping and reporting capabilities. The custodian may need to develop customized reporting systems to deliver reports for custody customers. These systems may include Internet access, dial-up access, and on-line trading terminals. National banks should carefully review their customers' reporting and recordkeeping requirements to ensure that they have the systems capability to provide the necessary services in an adequate manner.

Recordkeeping requirements for custodians extend beyond the normal requirements for tax reporting and financial accounting. National banks are required to maintain records in connection with the Bank Secrecy Act; recordkeeping and confirmation requirements for securities transactions, as required by 12 CFR 12, and other applicable laws related to record retention.

Custodians offering services in foreign countries must also observe the recordkeeping and reporting requirements of those countries.

Reporting and recordkeeping systems are important risk management tools. A national bank's custody systems should provide activity and exception reports that allow management to effectively identify and monitor the risks in its custody operations.

Cash Management

Cash management is a service provided to customers involving moving, managing, and monitoring cash positions associated with securities transactions. Cash management responsibilities should be clearly defined in the custody contract or a separate agreement. Services provided include investment of excess cash, online review of cash balances and projections, and facilitation of foreign exchange and hedging activities.

Excess cash is invested in such vehicles as time deposits, money market funds, short-term investment funds, and interest-bearing accounts in a variety of currencies. A custodian typically does not have discretion to select the investment vehicles; standing instructions in the custody agreement usually direct that selection.

Pooling and sweeping are common cash management product offerings. Pooling allows customers to net cash positions in various locations (and in various currencies), ultimately pooling the net result into a single central fund. Sweeping places the net cash into a designated money market fund for investment. In addition, some countries have restrictions on paying interest on certain types of accounts. Custodians may move cash from those accounts offshore to earn interest payments legally.

Foreign Exchange

Global custodians may provide foreign exchange (FX) services to facilitate settlement of cross-border securities transactions. The custody agreement should require customers to authorize foreign currency transactions, either by transaction or through the use of standing instructions. If the standing instructions do not direct the custodian to execute an FX transaction or a forward transaction, the customer should accept the risk of currency fluctuations prior to settlement. Foreign exchange services may also be used to facilitate a customer's currency hedging activities. For information on foreign currency transactions, please refer to the "Risk Management of Financial Derivatives" booklet of the *Comptroller's Handbook*.

When standing instructions are used for an ERISA account, and the transactions are executed through the custodian's foreign exchange desk, special restrictions may apply. Prohibited Transaction Exemption (PTE) 98-54, issued by the Department of Labor on November 13, 1998, granted a class exemption for custodians using their own foreign exchange desks to execute foreign currency transactions pursuant to standing instructions.

Securities Servicing

Securities servicing is a "core" ongoing service provided by custodians. This service includes collecting dividends and interest payments, processing corporate actions, and applying for tax relief from foreign governments on behalf of customers.

Income Collection

Custodians are responsible for collecting income payments received from the assets held under custody. The income payments typically take the form of dividends on equity securities and interest on bonds and cash equivalents. Custodians inform customers of projected income payments, enabling the customers to make their cash productive as soon as possible.

The bank's internal controls for income collection should include an income map (multi-account posting procedure) that details each client's expected income from a particular security. The bank should have income suspense (house) accounts that are used to process income payments that do not agree with forecasted projections.

In the United States, custodians commonly post income payments to customers' accounts on the payable date or the next day. This may be referred to as a contractual payment basis rather than an actual payment basis. Contractual income payments are posted to the customer's account on the date they are due rather than the date they are received by the custodian. Contractual income payments are not offered in all markets or for all products.

Corporate Actions

A corporate action is an event related to capital reorganization or restructures affecting a shareholder. Examples of corporate actions include rights issues, stock dividends, stock splits, and tender offers. Refer to appendix B for a list of common types of corporate actions.

Custodians are responsible for monitoring corporate actions for the securities they hold under custody. The contract should clearly define the responsibilities of each party involved in processing corporate actions. The custodian is typically notified of corporate actions by a vendor data feed; however, in some emerging markets the custodian relies on a sub-custodian to monitor corporate actions within its market. Once the custodian is notified of a corporate action, it identifies which accounts hold the security. If the account holder has a specified time to decide whether to accept the corporate action, the customer should be promptly contacted. The custodian should have a process to monitor the corporate action to ensure that the customer has given a complete response by the due date. When a customer's instructions are received, the custodian sends the instructions to the company (or in the case of a foreign corporate action, to the sub-custodian) for execution. The custodian monitors the status of the action to ensure timely settlement.

When a bank processes corporate actions ineffectively, it can lose money. For example, when a bank fails to notify customers that a corporate action is proposed to which they must respond, the bank may end up compensating customers for causing them to miss a money-making opportunity. Every custodian should have systems to make it aware of all corporate actions for assets under custody, to track customer notifications and time frames, and to process and settle the actions in a timely manner. The custodian's procedures for corporate actions should include documentation of all customer directions.

Processing corporate actions of corporations in foreign countries holds higher risk than processing the actions of domestic corporations. Most foreign markets are less automated than those in the United States; the possibility of delays is greater from the start. Types and definitions of corporate actions may differ from one market to the next, and clarification may be needed. Documents received in a foreign language may have to be translated since there currently is no global messaging standard. The complex legal provisions of the corporate actions of American companies are difficult to interpret, and they're written in English; how much more difficult such complex provisions are to interpret if they're, say, based on Japanese law and written in Japanese. To mitigate risks in this area, banks should have an experienced staff and access to legal counsel. Custody agreements should establish duties and responsibilities relating to corporate actions, including who is liable if actions are missed or misinterpreted.

Tax Reclaims

Many countries impose withholding taxes on dividends and interest payments to nonresident investors. Custodians may provide a service to minimize foreign withholding taxes or reclaim taxes withheld for their customers. (Nonresidents generally are not taxed on capital gains on the proceeds of the sale of a foreign security, but there are exceptions.) These services are provided not just by global custodians but also by U.S. custodians with nonresident alien (NRA) customers.

Tax treaties between countries often reduce withholding taxes and exempt capital gains from taxes. The purpose of tax treaties is to reduce the possibility of double taxation on income earned in foreign countries. In addition, some countries provide reduced tax withholding rates for certain types of investments (government bonds, for example) or for certain types of investors (investors exempt from taxation in their home country, for example).

Tax treaty benefits may provide for reduced withholding tax at the time the interest or dividend is paid ("relief at source"), while other treaties may require the investor to file for a refund after the fact ("reclaim"). To obtain relief at source, the custodian generally has to file a form or statement on behalf of the client, certifying the investor's tax status and country of residence for tax purposes. To reclaim excess withholding tax, a custodian generally is required to file a form with a country's tax authority. Some tax authorities may require the beneficial owner of the securities to sign this refund claim. The documentation requirements, time frames for filing, and other regulations vary depending on the treaty and the country's taxation rules. A custodian must know the tax rates for each of the countries in which it provides custody. Dividends, interest, and capital gains may all be taxed at different rates. The custodian also must know what tax treaties are in force within its custody network, and whether its customers qualify for relief under the treaty. For each country in which a custodian operates, the custodian must maintain information on the availability of reduced withholding rates for certain investors or for certain types of investments. Problems a custodian may face in dealing with foreign tax reclaim issues include:

- Obtaining updated information from foreign tax authorities.
- Language barriers.
- Statutes of limitation on filing tax reclaims.
- Length of time required to obtain refunds (some countries process reclaims only once per year).
- Requirements that claims be filed at the individual/beneficial owner level rather than on a commingled/omnibus account basis.
- Tax status of different investors.

A custodian should have a process in place to monitor the tax reclaim process. All necessary documentation should be obtained from the customer when the custody relationship is established. Income should be monitored for tax withheld, and a system should be established for submitting tax reclaims to foreign taxation authorities, monitoring the status of pending reclaim items, and following up on items outstanding for longer than the normal market time frames.

Securities Lending

Securities lending has evolved into one of the most important value-added products custodians offer to their customers. Bank custodians have traditionally acted as the lending agent for customers' securities lending activities; however, because the securities lending market is extremely competitive, third-party intermediaries have emerged. Wholesale intermediaries conduct transactions directly with the lender and the borrower, becoming a principal to the transaction. Niche intermediaries may specialize in particular types of securities loaned or aggressive cash collateral reinvestment programs. Third-party intermediaries may target clients that are dissatisfied with the performance of their custody banks. Internet auction systems for securities lending are being started up. These auctions, which bring lenders and borrowers together, may eliminate custodian and third-party intermediaries. The discussion in this section is limited to a custodian's role as lending agent for its customer.

The Evolution of Securities Lending Markets

The securities lending markets have existed in the United States since the 1960s, when an active inter-dealer market developed. In the 1970s, U.S. custodian banks first began lending securities to brokers on behalf of their clients. Demand for securities lending increased as new forms of trading strategies emerged. In 1982, the collapse of a U.S. securities dealer led to a number of reforms, including standardized agreements and collateral margins. The 1980s also saw a dramatic increase in the size of government securities markets in the United States and many other countries. Growth of securities lending in some foreign markets was hampered by concerns about the legalities of transactions, unfavorable tax treatment, and assorted regulatory restrictions. This resulted in the development of "offshore" securities lending markets, where securities lending transactions were settled on the books of foreign sub-custodians. This offshore activity fed increasing demand for non-U.S. securities. In the 1990s as growth of securities lending continued, such lending expanded into emerging markets. In the wake of this growth, many foreign markets have worked to address legal, tax, and regulatory issues impeding securities lending activities.

The globalization of securities markets, the consolidation of financial intermediaries, and shortened settlement cycles will have a significant impact on how the industry continues to evolve. These industry developments are designed to lend efficiency and innovation to the market, and will present a challenge for custodians maintaining a securities lending strategy.

The Role of Bank Custodians

Custodian banks have traditionally been the primary lending agent or intermediary, bringing borrowers and lenders together for a fee. Custodians require a large base of lendable assets to make their securities lending program profitable. Other portfolio-related factors that may affect the success of a bank's securities lending program are:

- Portfolio composition. If the portfolio is made up of securities widely available in the market, the demand for those securities may be low, making it difficult to locate a borrower. In contrast, a portfolio made up of "specials" or securities in high demand will be easy to lend.

- Portfolio management style. A portfolio that is actively managed is generally less attractive to borrowers than a passively managed portfolio because its turnover is likely to be higher. High turnover can lead to inconvenient recalls of loaned securities.

In addition to providing the lendable assets, custodians typically provide settlement services for the securities lending transaction, and safekeeping and/or investment management services for the collateral. These functions are discussed in the "Settlement and Safekeeping" sections above, and in the "Collateral Management" and "Operations" sections below.

Finders

Finders are fully disclosed intermediaries who bring lenders and borrowers together. If the bank is a finder, the bank will receive either a finder's fee (flat fee) or a revenue-based fee. Some banks may use a finder to attract securities lending customers. A bank using a finder should have written policies covering the circumstances in which a finder will be used, which party pays the fee (borrower or lender), and which finders the institution will use.

The Securities Lending Transaction

A securities lending transaction is essentially the temporary, collateralized loan of securities by the owner (lender) to a borrower, for a fee. Securities lending adds liquidity and efficiency to the markets, and supports trading activities and strategies in the United States as well as other major markets.

Parties to the Transaction

Lenders of securities are typically institutional investors with large investment portfolios such as mutual funds, pension plans, insurance companies, and endowments. The primary borrowers of securities are broker-dealers.

Reasons Parties Engage in Securities Lending

Borrowers may engage in securities lending for a variety of reasons, but primarily to cover short sales or failed trades, or to execute hedging or arbitrage strategies. Lenders engage in securities lending transactions as a means of increasing the incremental yield on their investment portfolios.

Transfer of Legal Title and Benefits

The legal title to the securities loaned passes to the borrower for the term of the loan. The lender regains title when the securities are returned. Although the lender temporarily loses legal ownership, the economic benefit of any corporate actions or income payments connected with the security on loan are retained through the use of "manufactured payments" from the borrower to the lender. However, the lender loses any voting rights associated with the security during the term of the loan. The legal rights and obligations of the parties should be set out in written agreements. Refer to the "Due Diligence" section below for additional information.

Collateral

The primary forms of collateral used for a securities lending transaction are cash, securities, or a standby letter of credit. If cash is provided as collateral, the lending agent or intermediary (e.g., the custody bank) will typically be responsible for investing the cash for the term of the loan. Providing cash collateral is the prevalent market practice in the United States. When securities are provided as collateral, the lender will typically specify the type of securities that are acceptable (e.g., government securities, minimum credit rating). Use of securities as collateral is common in most non-U.S. markets. Value of the collateral provided generally exceeds the value of the securities loaned. Collateral margins are discussed further in the "Collateral Management" section below.

Fees

The fee paid by the borrower will depend on the type of collateral for the loan. The fee may also vary with the supply and demand for the security borrowed. If the collateral for the loan is a security or a letter of credit, the borrower will pay a negotiated fee to the lender. If cash secures the loan, the borrower receives a negotiated rate of return (the rebate rate) on the collateral. The rebate rate is typically based on benchmark rates such as the Fed Funds rate, the Repo rate, or LIBOR. The lender is entitled to retain any income earned on the reinvestment of the cash collateral in excess of the rebate rate. Typically, the lender and the lending agent (custodian) split the excess income.

Due Diligence Considerations

A national bank should have board-approved securities lending policies (or ones approved by a designated committee) in place prior to engaging in securities lending activities. The custodian bank should ensure that written agreements are in place with potential borrowers, and with customers participating in the securities lending program. Due diligence reviews should be conducted on potential borrowers, and counterparty credit limits should be established.

Loan Agreement

The bank should have a written agreement in place before engaging in a securities lending transaction with a borrower. Master agreements, which detail the duties and responsibilities of each party, were initially developed to manage risks resulting from a broker failure. In the United States, the most widely used securities lending agreement is the Master Securities Loan Agreement published by the Bond Market Association (formerly known as the Public Securities Association). The most widely used global master securities lending agreement is the Overseas Securities Lending Agreement. Banks in all G-10 countries use master agreements to establish terms and conditions, as well as to manage risk. Some banks use standard agreements developed in-house; others negotiate each agreement.

At a minimum, the written agreement with the borrower should address:

- Transfer of legal title, structure of the transaction;
- Length of the loan;
- Acceptable forms of collateral and margin requirements;
- Valuation of collateral and margin calls;
- Manufactured payments;
- Rebate rates or other fees;
- Termination of the loan and return of securities; and
- Events of default.

Banks should use master or standard agreements whenever possible. A bank's legal counsel should thoroughly review each master and standard agreement and all securities lending arrangements that do not use the bank's standard documents.

Agency Agreement

It is important that the bank have written agreements with all customers that clearly delineate the duties and responsibilities of the bank as the customer's lending agent. At a minimum, the agreement should address:

- Acceptable forms of collateral and margin requirements;
- Reinvestment of cash collateral;
- Fee schedule;

- Approval of borrowers;
- Indemnification, if applicable;
- Termination of the loan; and
- Events of default.

A customer may use the agreement to customize its securities lending program. For example, the customer can establish its own cash collateral investment guidelines or may limit acceptable borrowers to those with a minimum credit rating.

A national bank may provide indemnification to its customers against risks associated with securities lending. When a bank offers indemnification, it assumes additional risks that should be reflected in the pricing. It is common for a bank to offer indemnification against borrower default. Indemnification against other types of risk, such as settlement risk, is less common. Indemnification should be addressed in the agency agreement.

Selection of Borrowers
The reputation risk associated with a borrower's default may be significant. The bank should have a well-developed, independent process in place to select borrowers. Once approved, borrowers should be reviewed periodically. Many bank custodians rely on bank credit departments to analyze the credit risk of their borrowers. Factors that should be considered during selection and ongoing review of a borrower include:

- Financial condition and capital adequacy;
- Risk profile, including an evaluation of how the borrower typically uses borrowed securities; and
- The borrower's reputation.

The bank should establish a credit limit for each borrower. The limit should be based on the bank's total exposure to the borrower, not just the exposure arising from the securities lending program.

Laws and Taxation

The laws and taxation applicable to securities lending transactions may vary significantly from market to market.

Legal Constraints on Some Lenders

A customer's participation in a securities lending program may be affected by statutory or regulatory restrictions. The most common example is a U.S. pension account that is subject to ERISA.

The Department of Labor (DOL) allows qualified employee benefit plans subject to ERISA to participate in securities lending programs if certain conditions are met. Prohibited Transaction Exemption (PTE) 81-6 details those conditions. In general, the conditions required by the DOL conform to industry standards.

A bank may act as a lending agent and receive reasonable compensation from covered plans provided the loan of securities is not prohibited by section 406(a) of ERISA. PTE 82-63 authorizes the lending agent to engage in securities lending on behalf of a plan and receive reasonable compensation paid in accordance with a written agreement. However, an independent plan fiduciary must grant prior written authorization for the compensation and may terminate such compensation upon written advance notification.

Other accounts that may be subject to regulations affecting securities lending transactions include own bank collective investment funds, affiliated mutual funds, and affiliated insurance companies. As part of its account acceptance process, a bank should identify any legal constraints on a customer's ability to participate in the securities lending program.

Tax Considerations

Section 1058 of the U.S. Tax Code provides participants in a securities lending arrangement with relief from recognition of gains and losses on the transfer of securities. Three requirements must be met to obtain this relief:

- The borrower must return securities to the lender that are identical to those borrowed.
- The borrower must, under the terms of the agreement, make payments to the lender that equal all dividends, interest, and other distributions to

which the owner of the securities is entitled during the period the securities are loaned.

· The terms of the agreement cannot reduce the lender's risk of loss or opportunity for gain on the security.

Tax treatment of loaned securities is complex and may affect a lender's holding period and basis in a security. National banks should have qualified tax professionals review their lending program to ensure that it meets the requirements of the tax code and any Internal Revenue Service regulations. If a bank offers securities lending in non-U.S. markets, local tax regulations should be researched for their impact on the bank's securities lending program.

Collateral Management

A national bank's collateral management process should address risk related to collateral margins, investment of cash collateral, and liquidity. Industry practice is to require collateral in excess of the market value of the securities loaned. Collateral margins may vary by market, and by type of collateral provided. In the United States, if cash or U.S. securities are provided as collateral, 102 percent of the value of the securities loaned is generally required. If non-U.S. securities are provided, 105 percent is typically required. In the case of securities that have high market price volatility, the bank's risk management process should address the need for higher collateral margins. If the securities loaned are fixed income, standard collateral margins would be increased by accrued interest. The parties generally have the right to negotiate the required collateral margin.

Collateral Margins

The securities loaned and the collateral provided are marked to market daily. When collateral exceeds the required margin, the excess may be returned to the borrower. Alternatively, when the collateral value is less than the required margin, the borrower must provide additional collateral.

The parties will stipulate who is responsible for safekeeping the collateral; the lending agent bank is often selected for the job. Some borrowers may require that the collateral be kept with an independent third party. The party safekeeping the collateral may do that alone, or it may also be responsible for pricing the assets, making margin calls, and collecting income. Responsibilities should be clearly set out in the agency agreement.

Management of Cash Collateral

One of the primary risks a national bank faces in securities lending is managing cash collateral. The investment of cash collateral is the primary source of revenue from securities lending activities. The return in excess of the borrower rebate is split between the agent bank (or investment manager) and the lending account. Because of the fee-sharing arrangement, a bank may have an incentive to accept higher risk in managing cash collateral. To control this risk, cash collateral should be invested pursuant to written investment guidelines.

The bank should have a written investment policy addressing management of cash collateral. The policy should establish minimum investment guidelines including permissible types of securities, minimum credit quality standards, maturity and duration limits, maturity mismatches, and liquidity requirements. The board of directors or its designated committee should approve the policy. A lender may direct the bank to use the lender's own guidelines rather than the bank's guidelines. If so, the agency agreement should say so.

If several lending customers use the bank's investment policy guidelines, the bank may manage the customers' cash collateral in a pooled account. If a customer has separate, written investment guidelines, the bank will manage that customer's collateral in a segregated account. A bank may manage a combination of segregated and pooled accounts, depending on customer needs.

Liquidity

National banks are exposed to liquidity risk by the short-term nature of most security loans. The bank must maintain adequate liquidity in the cash collateral investments to meet the needs of both borrower and lender. The lender has the option of recalling loaned securities at any time (i.e., if they want to sell them). Many brokers clear securities lending positions off their books for their periodic accountings. On an overnight basis, brokers may return large quantities of borrowed securities, only to borrow them again the next day.

Management of Indirect Financial Risk

The investment guidelines (the bank's or the customer's) provide the framework for managing the interest rate, credit, price, and liquidity risks associated with managing cash collateral. The manner in which the bank manages these risks may affect the bank's reputation and strategic risk. The bank should have a system in place to identify, measure, monitor, and control the risk inherent in managing the cash collateral to ensure that the level of risk present is in compliance with customer's directions and the bank's internal risk tolerance. If the bank manages the cash collateral within the established policy guidelines, contractually it should not be liable for losses because of its management of cash collateral. However, in several highly publicized cases in the mid-1990s banks absorbed significant losses from the management of cash collateral to protect customer relationships and their own reputations.

Securities Lending Operations

An efficient and well-organized custody operation system is essential to a securities lending program. Bank systems should be capable of handling a large volume of transactions, initiating and settling trades, clearing fails, collecting income and dividends, pricing collateral and loaned securities, making margin calls, and providing multi-currency pricing. Banks must be willing to devote sufficient resources to technology to remain competitive.

General controls and processes for safekeeping and securities settlement are common to custody and securities lending activities. However, there are additional operational needs for securities lending activities that a national bank should consider:

· Loan scheduling/allocation.
· Mark-to-market program.
· Tracking income and corporate actions for securities on loan.
· Cash collateral management (custodian does not normally invest customer assets).
· When collateral is in the form of securities rather than cash, and there is no DVP mechanism, the common practice is to deliver the collateral 1-2 days prior to borrowing the security. On return, collateral is returned before the security.
· Foreign registration regulations may preclude the redelivery of foreign-registered securities.

Recordkeeping and MIS
Management's ability to manage, monitor, and control risks arising from securities lending activities depends on timely and accurate information.

Banks should have an automated reporting system that should at a minimum provide daily reports of exceptions, securities available for loan, securities on loan, valuation of cash collateral, daily mark-to-market information, and margin calls.

Allocation of Loans among Lenders
A national bank should have a process in place to allocate the loans fairly and equitably among the possible lenders for a particular security. The system should be independently tested when adopted or revised, and should be retested periodically thereafter. It is not sufficient for a bank to rely on testing performed by the software or system developer.

Regulatory Reporting
Securities lending and borrowing transactions must be reported in accordance with the FFIEC's "Instructions for the Consolidated Reports of Condition and Income."

International Securities Lending

Banks that offer international securities lending programs should have access to efficient global custody networks. The amount of transaction risk the bank may be exposed to increases commensurate with the difficulties experienced in settling trades and transferring collateral. Some of the issues to keep in mind when examining an international securities lending program include:

- Legal and regulatory environment. Determining applicable law and understanding the regulatory environment in each country in which a bank operates.
- Multi-currency pricing and valuations of securities loaned and collateral.
- Settlement of transactions, including the timing and transfer of securities loaned and collateral.
- Tax considerations.

Other Value-Added Services

As the automation of transaction processing continues, the core custody business is rapidly becoming a commodity business with accompanying low profit margins. The future of the custody business lies in the custodian being able to identify ways to enhance the investment process for its customers.

Risk Measurement and Management

Custodians are providing added value to their customers by offering a variety of risk management tools, including:

- Applications that monitor and identify exceptions to customer's internal investment portfolio guidelines or limits (e.g., country or sector weightings).
- Asset allocation tools, including scenario analysis and optimizers.
- Analyses of Value at Risk (VAR) and Risk Adjusted Return on Capital (RAROC).
- Strategic cash management services including interest rate analyses, mark-to-market pricing, and stress testing.

Compliance Monitoring

Many custody customers, such as pension funds and investment managers, must comply with rules established by regulation, prospectus, or investment committee. Custodians may provide these customers with products and services that facilitate compliance monitoring, testing, and reporting.

Performance Measurement

Custodians may be asked to provide performance measurement tools for customers that allow them to review performance by investment manager, or to review fund performance against benchmark portfolios. Performance attribution analysis and risk-adjusted performance measurement are also products that a custodian may offer.

Banks as Users of Custody Services

As the custody services industry continues to consolidate, the number of banks outsourcing custody of their customer assets has also increased. A bank that uses an external provider of domestic or global custody should have a due diligence process in place for selection of its custodian. Considerations should include:

- Financial condition.
- Position in the market.

- Annual Report on Policies and Procedures (SAS 70).
- Availability of sufficient MIS to allow the bank to monitor its securities, cash, and income positions.
- Reporting options for the bank's customer accounts.
- The extent of the provider's sub-custodian network.
- The provider's due diligence review process for its sub-custodian banks, and the frequency of its ongoing reviews.
- Compliance with SEC Rule 17f, when applicable.
- The provider's multi-currency accounting and reporting capabilities.
- Prohibition of security lending except by express direction of the bank.
- The ability to use any broker for trading.
- Fees.

The bank should ensure that proper controls are in place for sending instructions to its custodian. In addition, the bank should have policies in place requiring that cash and securities positions be reconciled regularly. The bank should also monitor MIS reports to ensure that exception items (such as failed securities transactions and nonreceipt of income) are promptly investigated and resolved.

Document Custody Services

The advent of the mortgage-backed and asset-backed securities industry created a need for document custodians. The primary sponsors of mortgage-backed securities programs are Ginnie Mae, Fannie Mae, and Freddie Mac. In addition, private financial institutions may sponsor nonqualifying mortgage-backed or asset-backed securities issues including residential mortgages, home-equity loans, commercial mortgages, student loans, credit cards, automobile loans, and leases.

National banks have entered the document custody services market. Banks provide initial, final, and recertification services for federal agencies and private issuers in accordance with contractual guidelines. Services include document safekeeping, inventory control, and loan warehousing.

National banks should develop effective systems to deal with the compliance, transactional, and reputation risks associated with document custody. Compliance systems should ensure that certifications are accurate and timely. Procedures should ensure that documents in a bank's control are adequately secured in a protected area. All document movements should be controlled and recorded. Inaccurate or delayed certifications and missing documents may result in monetary loss or loss of business. In extreme cases of noncompliance with agency guidelines, the agency may revoke a bank's ability to be a custodian for agency issues.

For additional information on agency certification requirements, please refer to guidance from Ginnie Mae, Fannie Mae, and Freddie Mac. Information on the mortgage banking and asset securitization processes can be found in the "Mortgage Banking" and the "Asset Securitization" booklets of the *Comptroller's Handbook*.

As of May 17, 2012, this guidance applies to federal savings associations in addition to national banks.*

Custody Services   Examination Procedures

General Procedures

These general procedures are intended to assist examiners in determining the adequacy of a bank's policies, procedures, and internal controls regarding custody services risk and risk management. The extent of testing and procedures performed should be based upon the examiner's assessment of risk. This assessment should include consideration of work performed by other regulatory agencies, internal and external auditors and other internal compliance review units, formalized policies and procedures, and the effectiveness of internal controls and management information systems (MIS).

Objective: To determine the scope of the examination of custody services and identify examination activities necessary to achieve the stated objectives.

1. Review the following documents to identify any previously noted problems that require follow-up:
    - Previous examination reports.
    - Examination conclusion comments.
    - Supervisory strategy.
    - EIC's scope memorandum.
    - Follow-up activities.
    - Work papers from previous examination.
    - Internal and external audit reports, and if necessary, audit work papers.

2. Obtain the following from the bank EIC:
    - Any useful MIS or other information obtained from the bank as part of the ongoing supervision process.
    - Any useful information obtained from the review of applicable board and committee minutes.
    - A list of board and executive or senior management committees that supervise custody services, including a list of members and meeting schedules. Also obtain the name and phone number of the person who maintains copies of minutes.
    - Reports related to custody services that have been furnished to any applicable committee or to the board of directors.

3.   Verify the completeness of requested information with the request list.

4.   Determine, during early discussions with management, whether there have been:
- Any significant changes in policies, procedures, computer systems, or personnel relating to custody activities or processes.
- Material changes in products, volumes, or market focus.
- Significant levels and trends for exceptions, fails, or losses for each custody services area.

5.   Review the bank's business and strategic plans and determine whether management's plans for the department are clear and reflect the current direction of the department.

6.   Using what you learned from these procedures and from discussions with the bank EIC, determine the scope of this examination and its objectives.

Custody Services   Quantity of Risk

Conclusion: The quantity of risk is (low, moderate, high).

Objective: To develop an overall conclusion on the quantity of risk, the examiner should first evaluate the quantity of transaction, compliance, credit, reputation, and strategic risks. Only after quantifying these risks should the examiner come to an overall conclusion on the quantity of risk.

Transaction Risk

Transaction risk is encountered in custody activities because of the high volume of transaction processing inherent in the business. A bank controls transaction risk by implementing a strong control environment.

Objective: To determine the quantity of transaction risk present in the bank's delivery and administration of custody services.

1.   Evaluate the products and services the bank offers. Consider:
    · New products.
    · New markets.
    · Changes in technology.

2.   Evaluate the total volume (both dollars and numbers) of transactions processed and the volume and age of exceptions. Consider:
    · Volume of transactions settled daily.
    · Percentage of transactions requiring manual intervention.
    · Percentage of transactions that fail (rejects, trade fails, etc.).
    · Volume and age of reconciling items.
    · Cash.
    · Securities by depository.
    · House accounts (suspense, receivables, taxes, etc.).

3.   Review the total market value of all assets held in custody services accounts. Consider both the size and number of accounts.

4.   Evaluate the significance of system and technology risks identified in IT audits, BIT reviews, and internal control reviews of the custody services area.

Compliance Risk

Banks offering custody services incur compliance risk through contractual relationships with customers as well as through the numerous applicable laws and regulations, both domestic and foreign.

Objective: To determine the quantity of compliance risk related to the bank's custody services activities.

1. Review the nature and extent of custody activities, including new products, services, and markets, that may have an impact on compliance risk.

2. Evaluate the volume and significance of litigation and customer complaints.

3. Evaluate the volume and significance of noncompliance and nonconformance with policies and procedures, laws, regulations, and prescribed practices.

4. Determine whether you must sample accounts to verify compliance with relevant laws and regulations. Consider identified weaknesses in internal control, audit, compliance, or risk management systems when making your decision.

Credit Risk

Credit risk is encountered in custody services activities when a counterparty does not fulfill its contractual part of a transaction, and the bank has to extend or commit its funds to complete the transaction.

Objective: To determine the quantity of credit risk present in the bank's delivery and administration of custody services.

1. Review the types and volumes of custody services products that require the bank to use a counterparty. Consider whether:

- Counterparty credit limits including daylight overdraft, pre-settlement, and settlement lines are appropriate.
- Credit risk is increasing or elevated because of services such as contractual settlement and contractual income payment.
- The bank is using settlement systems with irrevocable payments, with delivery commitment features, or where settlement is not DVP.
- The bank has conducted due diligence reviews of its third-party sub-custodians when it provides global custody services.
- The bank offers indemnification against borrower default or other credit risks when the bank offers securities lending.

2. Review the overdraft list to determine the size, age, and general trend of these items.

Strategic Risk

To evaluate strategic risk, an examiner should consider the levels of risk associated with a bank's custody services activities in relation to the bank's strategic objectives.

Objective: To determine the quantity of strategic risk present in the bank's delivery and administration of custody services.

1. Review the strategic plan for custody services and discuss with management the strategic objectives the bank has established for its custody activities. Consider the bank's:
   - Goals for revenue and net income growth.
   - Current technology capacity assessments.
   - Future technology needs.
   - Staffing.
   - New markets.

2. Determine whether any weaknesses were identified in other areas that may hamper the bank's ability to achieve its strategic goals.

Reputation Risk

A sound reputation is essential for a bank custodian. The examiner's estimation of the quantity of reputation risk depends upon the level of transaction and compliance risk and the quality of the bank's control systems.

Objective: To determine the quantity of reputation risk present in the bank's delivery and administration of custody services.

1. Review the transaction risk, compliance risk, and strategic risk factors to determine whether:
    · The bank's strategic plan is in place and being followed.
    · The control structure is appropriate for the volume and nature of the transactions processed.
    · The compliance and audit programs have adequate policies and procedures for the bank's custody business.
    · The bank's reputation has suffered from lawsuits, complaints, or losses caused by custody service.

Custody Services Quality of Risk Management

Conclusion: **The quality of risk management is (strong, satisfactory, or weak).**

Policy

Objective: To determine whether the board and senior management have provided management with guidance on strategic direction and the organizational structure of the bank's custody services.

1. Review minutes, resolutions, bylaws, or other documents to determine whether the board of directors or its designated committee has approved and periodically reviewed:
   - The strategic plan, strategic direction of the custody business, and budgeting process.
   - The organizational structure of the custody business, including delegation of the administration of the custody business to designated persons or committees.

2. Evaluate the bank's strategies for custody services products through discussion with management and a review of technology plans. Consider:
   - Whether custody services are consistent with the bank's overall mission, strategic goals, and operating plans.
   - The level of management's knowledge of the industry operating systems.
   - Whether management evaluates internal controls, security risks, and vulnerabilities.
   - The bank's internal expertise and technical training.
   - Management's attention to system security monitoring and testing.
   - Management's knowledge of and compliance with applicable laws, regulations, and interpretations as they pertain to custody services.

Objective: To determine the adequacy of policies on custody services.

1. Determine whether the bank-adopted policies incorporate internal controls, account acceptance, monitoring, new product approvals, and audit.

2.   Determine whether the bank has adopted policies and procedures specifically required by applicable law or regulation, including:
   · 12 CFR 12 — Recordkeeping- and confirmation requirements for securities transactions.
   · 12 CFR 21 — BSA program.
   · 17 CFR 240.17f-1 — Lost and Stolen Securities.
   · Other policies as required by applicable law.

Processes

Review the bank's custody services to determine whether the board and senior management have provided an adequate system of controls, procedures, and practices for administering the processes needed to perform its custody services.

Objective: To determine the effectiveness of the control processes for custody services.

Note: The adequacy and scope of the audit coverage may affect the level of examiner testing and sampling of custodial control activities. Whenever possible, evaluate the audit early in the examination process. Refer to the "Internal and External Audits" booklet of the *Comptroller's Handbook* for additional procedures.

1.   Evaluate audit's process review of custody services. Consider:
   · Whether the audit scope covers significant activities and controls.
   · The quality of the audit reports.
   · The independence of the audit function, including authority and reporting lines.

2.   Discuss with senior management its control process to gain an understanding of:
   · The control culture and structure.
   · The results of any control self-assessment including administrative reviews of custody accounts.
   · The control placed on high-risk custody processes (cash movements, asset movements, and corporate actions).
   · The availability of any independent tests of the control structure — audits, SAS 70 reviews, etc.

- Compliance reviews of processes and internal controls used.
- MIS processes used to control high-risk activities.

3. Determine whether logical access controls on computer systems adequately segregate duties. Does the process for monitoring logical access to all systems[2] include:
    - A review of job profiles for segregation of duties related to logical access needs (system to system)?
    - A timely review of all changes in logical access by independent personnel?
    - The prompt removal of logical access for terminated and transferred employees?
    - Notification of security personnel or senior management when emergency access (firecall) is used?

4. Determine the adequacy of the control processes and segregation of duties for assets held off-premises and on-premises. Consider:
    - Logical access controls (for offsite depositories and custodians) such as
        - Dual control procedures.
        - Independent free receipt and free delivery monitoring.
        - Independent daily position change verification.[3]
        - Independent monthly position verification.

    - Physical access controls such as
        - Dual control procedures.
        - Vault entry records.
        - Asset tickets.
        - Physical security measures.
        - Periodic vault counts.

5. Evaluate the bank's control process for monitoring the accuracy of the accounting controls for its custody services activities. Consider:
    - The promptness with which assets are posted to the system.
    - The process for managing routine and non-routine manual instructions.

---

[2] The "Separation of Duties Matrix" at the end of the procedures may assist you in performing this review.
[3] If the bank does not have active controls over free deliveries, an independent reconcilement of the changes in the depository should be performed each day a change in the asset position occurs.

- The process for confirming that posted debit and credit totals agree with posting totals (including rejects).
- The separation of duties between:
  - Data input and asset balancing functions.
  - Authorization and release of assets or funds.
- Periodic trial balances.
- The timeliness of independent reconcilement functions and exception reporting standards (includes aged items) regarding:
  - Reconcilement and review of DDA positions.
  - Reconcilement of assets held at each depository and other custodians.
  - Reconcilement and review of suspense (house) accounts.
  - Internal control standards for follow-up, resolution, and reporting standards for exceptions.
- The effectiveness of the charge-off policy.

6. Evaluate the bank's control process for house accounts, failed trades, and corporate actions. Consider whether:
   - House accounts are established only after senior management approves their stated purpose.
   - House accounts are reconciled and reviewed by independent personnel, and aged items have trigger dates for escalation to senior management.
   - All failed trades are appropriately processed and monitored.
   - The bank's control process for corporate actions includes testing for sufficiency by account and by units.
   - The control process for corporate actions includes trigger dates and monitoring by personnel independent of the processing function.

Objective: To determine the adequacy of the account acceptance process.
(Review any audit or compliance reports for coverage of account acceptance.)

1. Evaluate the adequacy of the processes for account acceptance and product development for custody services. Select a sample of new accounts received and determine whether:
   - The bank assessed the account's custody requirements including all affected departments.
   - Due diligence reviews include customer identification and expected transaction information.
   - The bank could lawfully service the account.

- The bank assessed the account's potential to be profitable.
- A committee or senior management received notice of the new account (including house accounts) and approved its acceptance.
- Any accepted account failed to meet one or more of the requirements of established bank policy.

Objective: To determine the adequacy of the management information system (MIS) process. (Review any audit or compliance reports for coverage of MIS.)

1. Determine the types and frequency of reports to management. Consider:
   - Transaction exception reports (failed trades, missed corporate actions, etc.).
   - Operational exception reports (out-of-balance errors).
   - Volume and efficiency reports.

2. Evaluate the bank's process for determining the adequacy of its custody information systems. Determine whether:
   - Critical applications or data are identified.
   - Security controls are defined.
   - Vulnerabilities associated with custody services are identified.

3. Determine the effectiveness of the bank's backup process and contingency planning process. Consider:
   - Frequency of data backups.
   - Location where backups are kept.
   - Disaster recovery plan. (See Banking Circular 177(revised).)
   - Testing of disaster recovery plan.
   - Review of MIS plans of third-party service bureau or outsourced vendor if applicable.

Objective: To determine the effectiveness of the processes designed to evaluate and manage outsourced functions or third-party (vendor) services used by custody services.

1. Evaluate the bank's risk assessment process for outsourced or vendor services. Consider whether:
   - Strategic and business plans are consistent with outsourcing activity.
   - Senior management and the board of directors are involved in outsourcing decisions and vendor selection.

---

2. Evaluate the bank's due diligence process in gathering and analyzing vendor information prior to entering into a contract. Determine whether management considers:
    · Vendor reputation.
    · Financial condition.
    · Costs for development, maintenance, and support.
    · Internal controls and recovery processes.
    · Establishing standards of service.
    · The vendor's insurance coverage.

3. Determine whether the bank has reviewed vendor contracts to ensure that the responsibilities of each party are appropriately identified and, for information systems, whether contracts address topics in the "Contracts" section of the *FFIEC Information Systems Examination Handbook.*

4. Determine whether the bank has a process for evaluating existing vendor services. Consider whether:
    · Management designates personnel responsible for vendor management.
    · Designated personnel are held accountable for monitoring ongoing activities and services.
    · The bank has an adequate process to ensure that software maintained by the vendor is under a software escrow agreement and that the file is regularly confirmed as current.

Objective: To determine the effectiveness of the processes designed to ensure compliance with applicable laws. Consider the following:

Securities Transaction Recordkeeping Rules — 12 CFR 12
1. Determine whether the bank maintains the following minimum records with necessary detail (12 CFR 12.3):
    · Chronological records.
    · Account records.
    · Memorandum or order ticket.
    · Record of broker/dealers.

2. Determine whether records are accurate and provide an adequate basis for audit (12 CFR 12.3(b)).

3. Determine whether the bank notifies the customer of transactions as required by 12 CFR 12.4 or by the alternative forms of notification in 12 CFR 12.5.

Shareholder Communications Rules

SEC Rules 17 CFR 240.14-17 govern the distribution of proxy materials and the disclosure of information about shareholders whose securities are registered in a bank nominee name.

1. Determine the process used by the bank to code accounts (OBO or NOBO)[4] to pass information received from issuers, such as proxies and annual reports, to beneficial owners as appropriate (17 CFR 240.14c-2 and 17 CFR 240.14c-101).

2. Review bank responses to requests for information from issuers to determine whether the responses were appropriate and timely (17 CFR 240.14b-2(b)).

U.S. Investment Company Assets — 17 CFR 240.17f

If the bank is the custodian of investment company assets, determine whether the processes to comply with SEC revised rule 17f-5 and new rule 17f-7 are adequate.

ERISA

If the bank is the custodian of retirement plan assets, determine whether the bank's process for receiving 12(b)(1) fees, shareholder servicer fees, or other fees is in compliance with ERISA guidelines. See Frost and Aetna letters (DOL Advisory Opinions 97-15A and 97-16A).

Free Riding — Regulation U — 12 CFR 221

Evaluate the bank's processes governing free-riding. (Refer to Banking Circular 275, "Free Riding in Custody Accounts.")

Bank Secrecy Act — 12 CFR 21.21 and 31 CFR 103

Review with EIC the extent of the custody services compliance review of BSA. If a BSA review of custody services needs to be performed,

---

[4] These codes denote whether a beneficial owner objects (OBO) or does not object (NOBO) to the disclosure of his or her name, address, and securities position.

refer to the "Bank Secrecy Act/Anti-Money Laundering" booklet of the *Comptroller's Handbook* for procedures.

Escheatment

Determine whether the bank's process for escheatment of unclaimed items is appropriate. Consider:

- Whether the bank ages outstanding checks, suspense account entries, or house accounts entries.
- Whether the bank filed escheatment reports with the proper jurisdiction.

Overdrafts — Regulation D — 12 CFR 204

Determine whether overdrafts are monitored and reported to the bank's comptroller for accurate reporting under Reg. D for reserve requirements.

Lost and Stolen Securities — 17 CFR 240.17f-1

Determine whether the bank has written procedures to report lost and stolen securities with the Securities Information Center (SIC). Consider whether:

- The bank is registered as a direct or indirect inquirer with SIC.
- The bank has a FINS number.

Other Applicable Laws

Determine through inquiry with senior management whether the bank has a process to determine the laws applicable to their custody services activities, and whether they have established processes to maintain compliance with them. Consider:

- State and local laws in the United States.
- Country laws governing sub-custodians in the network.
- Central securities depositories (CSD) requirements.
- Foreign tax regulations and reclaim practices.

Objective: To determine the effectiveness of the processes designed to ensure proper safekeeping and settlement.

Safekeeping of Custody Assets

1. Determine whether any further review of the safekeeping process is needed after reviewing the audit and control processes related to on-premises and off-premises safekeeping. Consider:
    - The scope of the audit coverage.
    - The size and nature (age) of exceptions reported.
    - Charge-offs due to lost or stolen securities.
    -

2. For global custody activities, determine whether the bank performs effective due diligence before entering a market. Consider:
    - Country risk.
    - The settlement environment.
    - Restrictions on foreign investment.
    - Investability of the market.
    - Availability and integrity of financial information.
    - Ability to perform services profitably.
    - Payment systems risk.

3. Determine whether the bank's due diligence process for selecting a global sub-custodian is appropriate. Consider whether:
    - The bank performed a review of the institution's financial strength and its insurance coverage.
    - The bank reviews the sub-custodian's position in and knowledge of the local market.
    - The bank determined that the sub-custodian has an adequate internal control environment.
    - The bank determined that the sub-custodian has an appropriate level of automation, and its plans for future systems development are adequate.
    - The quality and experience of the personnel were evaluated.
    - The global custodian is ensuring that the sub-custodian is complying with SEC Rule 17f in cases when the sub-custodian holds assets of a U.S. mutual fund.

Settlement

1. Evaluate the effectiveness of the process for settlement of trades. Consider whether:
    - Proper trade instructions are received.
    - Trade instructions are properly documented.
    - Trade tickets (or memoranda) are properly controlled and contain all required information.
    - Independent reconcilement of broker confirmations to trade tickets is done.
    - Failed trades are monitored.
    - Confirmations are sent as required and contain all necessary data.
    - Customer accounts are monitored to determine that the securities or cash needed for settlement are available.
    - Information and instructions from the depository agree with the custodian's securities movement and control system (SMAC).
    - Settlements are DVP.
    - Depository position changes are matched to the changes on the bank's accounting records.

2. For cross-border trades, determine whether, in addition to the processes above, the process for conducting foreign exchange (FX) is adequate. Consider:
    - FX and forward contract instructions for each trade or per standing instructions.
    - Indemnity for FX risk when the customer does not want to use FX or forward contracts.

Objective: To determine the effectiveness of the processes designed to ensure effective and efficient servicing of assets in custody and on loan.

1. Evaluate the income collection process based upon a review of the following:
    - The methods and services subscribed to that provide information (or forecasts) on income from custody assets (look closely into irregular payments such as asset-backed securities).
    - The internal control process, including maps, suspense accounts, and the suspense account monitoring and control process for processing income payments.
    - The process for aging items in the income suspense accounts. (Review for possible unclaimed property or escheatment issues.)

- Whether income payments are contractual or actual.
- The process for monitoring, verifying, and posting reinvested income (mutual funds, CDs, and OID issues).
- The process for managing fixed income premiums and discounts.

2. Evaluate the bank's corporate actions process. Consider whether:
   - The bank subscribes to a service that provides information about tender offers, mergers, called debt issues, and class actions.
   - Bonds are redeemed promptly.
   - The monitoring and call-back procedures on voluntary corporate actions are appropriate.
   - The bank uses a recorded line.
   - The procedures for domestic corporate actions and mini-tenders are adequate.
   - The monitoring process for each new corporate action is adequate.
   - The customers are properly notified about voluntary actions.
   - The response monitoring process includes balancing responses by customer count and by total par or shares (sufficiency).
   - The process to document customer responses on voluntary actions is adequate (high-level risk management process).
   - The review process for completed corporate actions is monitored.
   - The procedures for cross-border corporate actions are adequate. Although the process is the same as for domestic corporate actions, also consider:
     – The process for translation of documents received in a foreign language.
     – The experience of the staff and access to legal counsel.
     – The bank's process to limit liability for missed or misinterpreted actions.

3. Determine whether the process for addressing tax reclaims on foreign securities is appropriate. Consider whether the bank:
   - Obtains updated information from foreign tax authorities.
   - Effectively manages the language differences.
   - Monitors the statute of limitations on filing tax reclaims.
   - Effectively manages the length of time required to obtain refunds (some countries process reclaims only once per year).
   - Requires that claims be filed for individual/beneficial owners rather than for commingled/omnibus accounts.

Objective: To determine the effectiveness of the processes used to evaluate and monitor overdrafts in custody services.

1. Evaluate the overdraft process. Consider whether:
    · Overdrafts are aged and have appropriate escalation processes.
    · The size of the overdraft is part of the escalation process.
    · The reason for the overdraft is appropriate.
    · The overdraft process considers free riding.

2. Determine whether the bank has a process for identifying credit limits for overdrafts.

Securities Lending Activities

Objective: To determine whether appropriate systems and controls are in place for the bank's securities lending activities.

Selection of Borrowers
Evaluate the bank's due diligence process.[5] Consider whether:
· There is a process in place to ensure initial and ongoing borrower reviews.
· Borrower risk profiles are developed, including an evaluation of how the borrower typically uses the borrowed securities.
· Credit lines have been approved for each borrower.
· Monitoring processes are in place.

Loan Agreement with Borrower
1. Determine whether the bank's processes ensure that written agreements are in place for all borrowers. Consider whether:
    · A standard or master agreement is used for all borrowers.
    · Customized agreements are used and, if so, whether they are reviewed by counsel prior to execution.

---

[5] Large banks should consider coordinating this review with capital market and credit specialists.

2. Review a sample of agreements to determine whether they address the following:
   - Transfer of legal title and structure of the transactions.
   - Length of the loans.
   - Acceptable forms of collateral.
   - The frequency of repricing of loaned securities.
   - Margin requirements, including higher margin requirements for volatile securities.
   - Margin calls and return of excess collateral.
   - Manufactured payments.
   - Rebate rates or other fees.
   - Termination of loans (including recall).
   - Return of securities identical to those borrowed.
   - Events of default.

Agency Agreement with Lending Customer

1. Determine whether written agreements are in place for all customers participating in the securities lending program.

2. Review a sample of the agreements to determine whether they address:
   - Acceptable forms of collateral and margin requirements.
   - Reinvestment of cash collateral, including any lender specified investment guidelines.
   - Approval of borrowers or any restricted borrowers.
   - Fees/revenue split.
   - Indemnification (if applicable), and whether there is a limit/cap on indemnity.
   - Termination of the loan, including notification requirements for any recalls.
   - Events of default.

Legal and Regulatory Requirements

Determine whether the bank has a process to ensure compliance with:
   - The requirements of PTE 81-6 and PTE 82-63 covering lending securities for accounts subject to ERISA.
   - The requirements of the Investment Company Act of 1940 for investment company assets loaned.
   - Insurance regulations for insurance company assets loaned.
   - Other regulated industries.

Management of Cash Collateral

1. Determine whether the process established for the investment of cash collateral is adequate. Consider whether:
   - The bank has established guidelines that have been approved by the board or an authorized committee.
   - The lender's investment policy guidelines/restrictions are written, are reviewed/confirmed periodically, and do not conflict with the bank's guidelines unless approved by the board or an authorized committee.

2. Review the bank's process for monitoring compliance with the applicable investment guidelines for each account or cash collateral pool. Consider whether:
   - Exceptions are promptly identified and reported (to the investment manager, compliance officer, or a committee).
   - The process for pricing securities is adequate.
   - The cash-monitoring process ensures that all cash is fully invested.
   - The process for the calculation of returns is adequate.

Operational Controls

The general process for securities movement, dual control, daily reconcilement of transactions, trade processing, and monitoring of aged fails are addressed in previous procedures. The following process reviews relate to operational controls for securities lending activities.

1. Determine whether the operational control process for securities lending is adequate. Consider whether:
   - Securities are marked to market daily, and the updates are forwarded to monitoring personnel.
   - The bank's process for notifying management of margin calls, collateral returns, or recalls of securities on loan is appropriate.
   - The process to "buy in" when loaned securities are not returned within agreed-upon time frames is appropriate.
   - The bank has a process to monitor invested cash collateral for lenders.

2. Determine whether the bank has a process for tracking income (manufactured payments) and corporate actions on loaned securities. Consider whether the bank:
   · Notifies lending clients of dividend/corporate action items while stocks are on loan.
   · Monitors the receipt of manufactured payments from borrowers of securities on loan.

3. Determine whether the process for the allocation of loans is adequate. Consider whether:
   · The queuing mechanism considers equitable allocation of securities loans between lending accounts.
   · The allocation of recalls between borrowers is equitable.
   · The process allows for any lender preferences or restrictions.
   · The algorithms used in the process are reviewed and independently tested.

International Securities Lending

Although international securities lending is similar to domestic (U.S.) securities lending, several differences are addressed by the following procedures.

Determine whether the bank has a process to identify any legal, regulatory, tax, or other requirements of the jurisdictions in which they operate. Consider the adequacy of the bank's process to:
· Monitor credit risk in each jurisdiction.[6]
· Monitor restrictions/guidelines on collateral.[7]
· Ensure that corporate actions on securities loaned (and returned) are appropriately exercised.
· Obtain favorable tax treatment of securities lending transactions (as the bank would using Internal Revenue Code 1058 in the United States.)
· Meet local documentation requirements.

---

[6] Where there is no DVP mechanism, the common practice is to deliver the collateral one to two days prior to borrowing the security. On return, collateral is returned before the security. Parties are exposed to counterparty credit risk for the amount of the collateral during this time.
[7] In some countries, there may be restrictions on the investment of cash collateral or the type of acceptable collateral.

Objective: To determine whether the bank has an effective due diligence process for all "other value-added services."

Evaluate the bank's process for approving new custody services. Consider:
- New services being offered since the previous examination.
- The bank's process for including comments from all affected departments during the review of the new service.
- The bank's documentation of board or committee approval.

Objective: To determine the effectiveness of the bank's due diligence reviews when it uses the custody services of third-party vendors and servicers.

1. Evaluate the bank's selection process for third-party vendors or servicers to perform its custody services. Consider whether the evaluations include:
   - A financial review.
   - An internal control review.
   - Comments from the vendor's other clients.
   - A review of the vendor's insurance coverage.
   - The establishment of service-level standards in the agreement.

2. Evaluate the bank's process for ongoing review of third-party vendors and servicers. Consider:
   - The frequency of financial reviews.
   - Reports covering internal control reviews (SAS 70, audit, or other).
   - Evaluations of the vendor's performance against agreed-upon standards.

Personnel

Objective: Given the size and complexity of the bank, determine whether bank management and personnel display acceptable knowledge and technical skills to manage its custody services activities.

1. Using what you have learned from performing these procedures, evaluate the knowledge, communications, and technical skills of management and staff members.

2. Evaluate whether the staff size is sufficient to manage the volume of business conducted. Consider:
   - Overtime records.
   - Turnover.
   - Plans for further automation.
   - Strategic direction

Controls

Objective: To determine whether management has established and implemented an appropriate control system to address the levels of risk arising from its custody services activities.

1. Determine whether custody services activities receive a suitable audit. Consider:
   - The independence of the audit function, including authority and reporting lines.
   - The process for reviewing and approving the audit scope, plan, and frequency.
   - The risk assessment process.
   - The adequacy of audit management and staffing, including staffing levels and expertise.
   - The quality of audit reports and supporting workpapers.
   - The audit scope and whether all significant activities and controls are covered.

2. Evaluate management's supervision and control of custody services through audit reports, compliance reports, and MIS reports. As a part of this evaluation:
   - Consult with the examiner reviewing bank compliance to determine whether the compliance systems are effective.
   - Consult with the examiner reviewing internal/external audit to evaluate audit coverage of issues related to custody services.

- Assess management's responsiveness to weaknesses or deficiencies identified by the control systems.
- Determine whether the MIS systems are adequate for the nature and volume of business being conducted.

Custody Services   Conclusions

Objective: To communicate findings and initiate corrective action when policies, practices, procedures, objectives, or internal controls are deficient or when violations of law, rulings, or regulations have been noted in the bank's administration of its custody services activities.

1.   Provide the EIC with a brief conclusion regarding:
     · The adequacy of risk management systems, including policies, processes, personnel, and control systems.
     · Internal control deficiencies or exceptions.
     · Bank conformance with established policies and procedures.
     · Significant violations of laws, rules, or regulations.
     · Corrective action recommended for identified deficiencies.
     · The adequacy of MIS.
     · Quantity of risk and quality of risk management associated with custody services.
     · The overall level of compliance with applicable law, accepted industry standards, and bank policies and procedures, to assist the EIC in determining the compliance rating.
     · Other matters of significance.

2.   Identify significant risks. Assess the impact of custody services on the bank's aggregate risks and the direction of those risks. Examiners should refer to guidance provided under the OCC's large bank risk assessment program.
     · Risk Categories: Transaction, Reputation, Compliance, Credit, or Strategic.
     · Risk Conclusions: High, Moderate, or Low.
     · Risk Direction: Increasing, Stable, or Decreasing.

3.   Determine, in consultation with the EIC, whether the risks identified are of enough significance to bring them to the board's attention in the report of examination. If so, prepare items for inclusion in "Matters Requiring Attention" (MRA).
     · The MRA should cover practices that:
        – Deviate from sound principles and may result in potential financial liability if not resolved.
        – Result in substantive noncompliance with laws.

- The MRA should discuss:
  - Causes of the problem.
  - Consequences of inaction.
  - Management's commitment to corrective action.
  - The time frame and person(s) responsible for corrective action.

4. Discuss findings with bank management, addressing:
   - Adequacy of risk management systems, including policies, processes, personnel, and control systems.
   - Violations of law, rulings, regulations, or significant internal control deficiencies, emphasizing their causes and the potential for risks associated with custody service activities.
   - Recommended corrective action for deficiencies cited.
   - Bank's commitment to specific actions for correcting deficiencies.

5. As appropriate, prepare a brief comment on custody services for the report of examination. In general terms, address the following subjects:
   - Quantity of risk.
   - Quality of risk management.

6. Prepare a memorandum or update the work program with any information that will facilitate future examinations.

7. Update the OCC's electronic information system.

8. Organize and reference work papers in accordance with OCC guidance. Work papers should clearly and adequately support the conclusions reached.

Separation of Duties Matrix

Bank Name: Prepared By:
Location: Reviewed By:
Charter #   Date

Determine whether the duties of preparing input, processing, and reconciling are separate. The extent to which a bank can separate job responsibilities depends on the size of the operation and the sophistication of services provided.

F = Full access to move assets or delete assets from records
R = Reconciles position   I = Inquiry only

Individual's Name	Accounting System	DTCC	FED	DDA	Corr. Bank	Foreign Custodian	Other	Other

As of May 17, 2012, this guidance applies to federal savings associations in addition to national banks.*

Custody Services   Appendix A

Glossary

This glossary defines terms used by the custody and securities settlement industry. The definitions are not legally precise for all relevant jurisdictions. This glossary's use of a hyperlink to any Web site is not an endorsement of the web site by Office of the Comptroller of the Currency. This glossary's hyperlinks are included as a reference only and were current at the time of publication.

Some of the definitions are from glossaries in two papers published by the Bank for International Settlement's Committee on Payment and Settlement Systems: "Disclosure Framework for Securities Settlement Systems" (1997) and "Securities Lending Transactions: Market Development and Implications" (1999). For a copy of these papers, please see the BIS internet site. http://www.bis.org/

Automated Customer Account Transfer Service (ACATS)
A system that automates and standardizes procedures for the transfer of assets in customer accounts between brokers, banks, mutual funds, trusts, and other financial institutions. The National Securities Clearing Corporation developed ACATS in the mid-1980s in conjunction with the New York Stock Exchange and the National Association of Securities Dealers to address the industry's need to reduce delays and inconsistencies associated with manual processing of account transfers. Banks may access ACATS through a Depository Trust Corporation link or through the National Securities Clearing Corporation's Web site.

Actual settlement
Settlement that occurs when the seller has received the proceeds and the buyer has received the securities. See contractual settlement (in which a trade settles regardless of whether these events occur).

Affirmation/confirmation process
The transmission of messages among broker-dealers, institutional investors, and custodian banks regarding the terms of a trade executed for an institutional investor. The Depository Trust Corporation's Institutional

---

Delivery (ID) system is an example of an affirmation/confirmation. See matching, qualified vendor.

Beneficial owner
A person who does not have legal title but who enjoys the benefits of ownership.

Bilateral netting
Consolidating cash flows from two different contracts or instruments.

Book-entry securities
Securities that are transferred electronically. No physical certificates change hands. See dematerialization, immobilization.

Book-entry system
An accounting system that permits the electronic transfer of securities and does not require certificates to change hands. See dematerialization, immobilization.

Bridge
The term commonly used for the link between Euroclear and Clearstream that permits cross-system settlements of trades between participants.

Buy-in
A purchase of securities in the open market by a lender because the borrower cannot deliver the securities to the lender in accordance with the terms of the transactions. The borrower pays all costs related to the buy-in.

Cedel (See Clearstream International)
An international central securities depository founded in 1970 and headquartered in Luxembourg. Cedel was renamed Clearstream after a 1999 merger. http://www.clearstream.com/

Central securities depository (CSD)
An institution created to hold physical securities so that securities transactions can be processed by book entry. The depository immobilizes (dematerializes) physical securities. See dematerialization, immobilization.

Clearing House Automated Payment System (CHAPS)

The United Kingdom's electronic transfer system for sending same-day value payments from bank to bank. It was introduced in 1984, and has operated as a real-time gross settlement system since April 1996. In 1999, CHAPS began offering payment services in Euro as well as Sterling. Every CHAPS payment is unconditional, irrevocable, and guaranteed. http://www.apacs.org.uk

Clearing House Interbank Payments System (CHIPS)

An on-line, real-time, large-value fund transfer network. A same-day settlement multilateral netting system, it is the central U.S. clearing system for international transactions. All transactions settle in U.S. dollars. Originated in 1970, CHIPS is a private funds transfer network managed by the Clearing House Interbank Payments Company LLC (CHIPCo). CHIPCo is owned by CHIPS participants. http://www.chips.org

Clearance

The process of calculating the mutual obligations of the participants, usually on a net basis, for the exchange of funds and securities. Clearance may also refer to the process of transferring securities on the settlement date (a clearing system), also known as a securities settlement system.

Clearing agency

Section 3(a)(23)(A) of the Securities Exchange Act of 1934 defines a clearing agency as "any person who acts as an intermediary in making payments or deliveries or both in connection with transactions in securities or who provides facilities for comparison of data respecting terms of settlement of securities transactions, to reduce the number of settlements of securities transactions, or for the allocation of securities settlement responsibilities." 15 USC 78c(a)(23)(A).

Clearing system

See securities settlement system (SSS).

Clearstream International

Clearstream International is a settlement organization offering comprehensive service for bonds and equities both domestic and cross-border. The company was formed from the merger of Cedel International and Deutsche Börse Clearing. Its shareholders consist of the world's major financial institutions. Clearstream International has two subsidiaries – Clearstream Banking and Clearstream Services. http://www.clearstream.com

---

Collateral
An asset or third-party commitment that is accepted by the lender to secure an obligation of the borrower.

Continuous net settlement (CNS)
A method of clearing and settling securities that matches transactions to available securities and results in net receive or net deliver positions (and funds) at the end of the day (or settlement period). This method requires the use of a clearing house (e.g., the National Securities Clearing Corporation) and a depository (e.g., the Depository Trust Company). Participants' positions are continuously updated as transactions settle.

Contractual settlement
An arrangement whereby the customer is credited with the sale proceeds on the contractual settlement date regardless of whether the proceeds have been received. In the case of purchases, the customer's account will be debited on the contractual settlement date regardless of whether the securities have been received. If the securities or proceeds have not been received by an agreed-upon date, the transaction typically will be reversed. See actual settlement.

Corporate actions
Events typically related to capital reorganization or restructuring. Corporate actions frequently require notification of and response by the beneficial owner of the security. See **appendix B** for examples of corporate actions.

Counterparty credit limits
Limits set by a trading party to restrict the amount of its credit exposure to different counterparties.

CREST
CREST is the real-time gross settlement system for United Kingdom government bonds (Gilts), collective instruments (unit investment trusts, open-ended investment companies), and money market instruments, and also for United Kingdom and Irish corporate securities. Participants hold securities in uncertificated form (see dematerialization), and transfers are made DVP (at the same time payment is made) electronically. (See delivery vs. payment.)
http://www.crestco.co.uk

Cross-border settlement
Settlement that takes place in a country other than the country in which one or both of the trade counterparties are located.

Cross-border transaction
A transaction in a foreign security, or a transaction in a domestic security, when at least one trade counterparty is located outside the domestic market.

CUSIP
The numbering system used in the United States to identify issuers and issues of securities. The CUSIP system originated from the American Bankers Association's Committee on Uniform Security Identification Procedures. Numbers are assigned by the CUSIP Service Bureau, which is operated by Standard & Poor's. http://www.cusip.com

CUSIP International Numbering System (CINS)
CINS uses the CUSIP numbering format to identify international securities. See CUSIP, ISID.

Custodian
A bank or other financial institution that provides safekeeping services and administers securities for its customers.

Custody
The safekeeping, settlement, and servicing of securities for customers.

Daylight overdraft
Credit extended for less than one business day. For example, in a clearing system with end-of-day final settlement, intra-day credit is extended by a participant that accepts and acts on a payment order, even though that participant will not receive final funds until the end of the business day.

Default
Failure to complete a funds or securities transfer according to its contractual terms for reasons that are not technical or temporary in nature. The reason is often a counterparty's bankruptcy or insolvency. Default is usually distinguished from a failed transaction.

Delivery
Final transfer of a security or financial instrument.

Delivery versus payment (DVP)
The International Securities Services Association defines DVP as simultaneous, final, irrevocable, and immediately available exchange of securities and cash on a continuous basis throughout the day. The Bank for International Settlement defines DVP as a link between a securities transfer system and a funds transfer system that ensures that delivery occurs if, and only if, payment occurs.

Dematerialization
The elimination of physical certificates or documents representing ownership of securities so that the securities exist only as accounting records. See book-entry securities, immobilization.

Depository receipt
An instrument issued in one country that establishes an entitlement to a security held in custody in another country. For example, American Depository Receipts (ADRs), which are receipts for shares of foreign-based corporations, are traded on U.S. exchanges; however, the underlying foreign shares are held in custody outside the United States.

The Depository Trust & Clearing Corporation (DTCC)
A holding company established in September 1999 to oversee two principal subsidiaries: the Depository Trust Company and the National Securities Clearing Corporation. http://www.dtcc.com

The Depository Trust Company (DTC)
A participant-owned central securities depository in the United States and a subsidiary of DTCC. DTC is a national clearinghouse for the settlement of trades in corporate and municipal securities. It performs custody services for its bank and broker/dealer customers. DTC products and services include:
- DTC Hub. DTC's centralized communications system that consolidates messages between institutional investors and bank custodians.
- Institutional Delivery (ID) System. DTC's confirmation/affirmation service.
- Standing Instruction Database (SID). A database which provides the participants' account and settlement instructions for all security types, settlement locations, and currencies. http://www.dtc.org

DK (Don't Know)

An explanation, in industry shorthand, of a custodian's refusal to accept a security delivery. DK means that the custodian does not know about the security and is not expecting it. Disagreement between parties on sale price, quantity, and other factors can also lead to a DK.

Domestic settlement

A settlement that takes place in the country where both counterparties to the trade are located.

Domestic trade

A trade between counterparties located in the same country.

Employee Retirement Income Security Act (ERISA)

A 1974 federal law governing most private pension and benefit plans.

Electronic Trade Confirmation (ETC)

A process providing an efficient bridge between pre-trade messaging and settlement processing. The industry views the role of ETC as crucial to achieving straight-through processing. Providers of ETC systems include DTC's ID system, Thomson Financial's OASYS, Financial Management Corporation's FMCNET, and ISMA's TRAX system.

Euroclear

An international central securities depository operated by the Brussels branch of Morgan Guaranty Trust Company of New York through the Euroclear Operations Center. Euroclear is owned by its participants.
http://www.euroclear.com

European Central Securities Depository Association (ECSDA)

An association of central securities depositories formed in 1997 to facilitate the exchange of ideas and collaboration on projects of mutual interest.
http://www.ecsda.com

Ex-dividend

The interval between the announcement of a dividend and the dividend's payment. An investor purchasing a security while it is ex-dividend is not entitled to the dividend.

Failed transaction
A securities transaction that fails to settle on the contractual settlement date because one of the counterparties fails to perform. The trade, which usually fails because of technical or temporary difficulties, often settles at a later date.

Fedwire
A Federal Reserve Bank transfer system with two components, Fedwire Funds Transfer Service and Fedwire Book-Entry Securities Service.
Fedwire Funds Transfer Service is a large-value funds transfer system that offers real-time gross settlement. Transfers are initiated by the sender.
Fedwire Book-Entry Securities Service is a large-value transfer system that offers real-time gross settlement and that operates on a delivery vs. payment system. Used for the safekeeping and transfer of U.S. government securities in book-entry form. Transfers are initiated by the sender of securities.
Once authorized (matched) and processed, all transfers are final.
http://www.federalreserve.gov/PaymentSystems/FedWire

Final transfer
An irrevocable and unconditional transfer which discharges the obligation to deliver or pay. See provisional transfer.

Financial Information Exchange (FIX)
A messaging protocol developed for the real-time electronic exchange of securities transaction information. FIX is popular with fund managers, broker-dealers, and institutional investors. http://www.fixprotocol.org

Free delivery
Securities delivered without a corresponding receipt of funds.

Free riding
A term for the practice of buying and selling securities, usually on the same day, in amounts greatly exceeding the amount allowed under margin collateral requirements. The practice is also referred to as "day trading." The free rider attempts to profit from short-term changes in market prices without placing significant personal funds at risk. This practice may result in a violation of 12 CFR 221 (Regulation U), and is addressed by OCC Banking Circular 275, "Free Riding in Custody Accounts," September 3, 1993.

Fungible
Freely exchangeable for or replaceable by similar securities or goods in the satisfaction of an obligation.

Global custodian
An institution that provides its customers with safekeeping services and that administers securities that trade and settle throughout the world.

Global Straight Through Processing Association (GSTPA)
An industry association of investment managers, broker/dealers, and global custodians involved in the processing of cross-border trades. The primary objectives of the GSTPA are to accelerate the flow of cross-border trade information, to reduce the number of failed cross-border trades, and to reduce the risks and the costs of cross-border trade settlements.
http://www.gstpa.org

Gross settlement system
A transfer system in which funds are settled or securities are transferred instruction by instruction.

Group of Thirty (G30)
A private, nonprofit international organization composed of representatives from the public sector and the private sector, including academia. The Group's objectives are to deepen the understanding of international financial and economic issues. In 1989, the G30 made recommendations regarding international clearance and settlement systems. http://www.group30.org

Immobilization
Placement of certificated securities and financial instruments in a central securities depository to facilitate book-entry transfers.

Indemnification
An agreement to compensate for damage or loss. Custodians may indemnify customers that lend securities.

Industry Standardization for Institutional Trade Communications (ISITC)
A working committee of securities operations professionals that defines message standards governing communications between custodians, investment managers, custodians, and broker/dealers and vendors. The ISITC's mission is to foster alliances and advocate standards that promote

straight-through processing (STP) of securities transactions.
http://www.isitc.org

Institutional Delivery (ID) System

A trade confirmation and affirmation system provided by the Depository Trust Corporation. Sometimes referred to as DTC-ID.

Internal settlement

A settlement that is effected through transfers of securities and funds on the books of a single intermediary. An internal settlement requires both counterparties to maintain their securities and funds accounts with the same intermediary.

International Central Securities Depository (ICSD)

A central securities depository that settles trades in international and domestic securities, usually through direct or indirect (through local agents) links to local central securities depositories. Customers include commercial and central banks, custodians, and broker/dealers.

International Organization of Securities Commissions (IOSCO)

The primary objectives of IOSCO are to promote high standards of regulation in order to maintain just, efficient, and sound markets; to establish standards and an effective surveillance of international securities transactions; and to promote the integrity of the markets by applying standards rigorously and enforcing them effectively. http://www.iosco.org

International Securities Identification Directory (ISID and ISID*Plus*)

Directory which includes CUSIP numbers and International Securities Identification Numbers, as well as cross-references to other international securities numbering systems. ISID*Plus* is produced jointly by Standard and Poor's and Telekurs (USA). http://www.isidplus.com

International Securities Identification Number (ISIN)

The ISIN provides a uniform structure for use in the trading and administration of securities in the international securities industry. The Euroclear Operations Center has been designated as the numbering agency for international securities.

International Securities Market Association (ISMA)
An industry organization based in Zurich, ISMA acts as a forum for questions related to international securities markets.

International Securities Services Association (ISSA)
An international organization of participants in the global securities markets including banks, clearing organizations, central securities depositories, broker/dealers, and asset managers. ISSA's stated goals include increasing knowledge of participants, improving communications, and promoting progress in the securities services industry. http://www.issanet.org

Irrevocable transfer
A transfer that the transferor cannot revoke.

Lamfalussy Standards
A report on netting schemes, issued in 1998, which advanced minimum standards for netting systems. In common references, the recommended standards took the name of the chairman of the committee issuing the report.

Legal ownership
Recognition in law as the owner of a security or financial instrument.

Local agent
A local custodian that provides custody services to nonresident trade counterparties and settlement intermediaries. Also known as a sub-custodian or agent bank.

Local custodian
Provides custody services for securities traded and settled in the country in which the custodian is located.

Loss-sharing agreement
An agreement among participants in a clearing or settlement system on how to allocate losses arising from the default of a participant in the system or from the default of the system itself.

Loss-sharing pools
Cash, securities, or other assets that are provided by the participants in advance and are held by the system to ensure that commitments arising from loss-sharing agreements can be met.

Manufactured payment

A payment from a borrower of securities compensating the lender of the securities for dividends or other income the lender would have received from the loaned securities.

Margin

The amount or percentage by which the collateral's value exceeds the value of securities on loan. Margin sometimes refers to the total value of collateral as a percentage of the loan value (e.g., 102 percent). Margin serves to reduce replacement cost exposures resulting from changes in market prices. Initial margin is deposited at the start of the transaction. Variation margin is called during the life of the loan if the value of the collateral falls below the initial margin requirement.

Margin call

A demand for additional funds or collateral, following the marking to market of securities involved in a loan, if the market value of the underlying collateral falls below a certain level relative to the loaned asset. If the value of the underlying collateral, following its revaluation, exceeds the agreed-upon margin, the lender may be required to return some of the collateral.

Marking to market

The practice of revaluing securities and financial instruments using current market prices.

Master agreement

An agreement that sets the standard terms and conditions on a securities lending transaction.

Matching

The process by which an intermediary compares the trade or settlement details provided by the broker-dealer with those of its customer. If the details match, the intermediary affirms the trade and a confirmation is generated. The SEC has interpreted matching as a "clearing agency function" according to the definition of a clearing agency in the Securities Exchange Act of 1934. See clearing agency, confirmation/affirmation process.

Multilateral netting

Netting among more than two parties.

National Securities Clearing Corporation (NSCC)

Provides centralized clearance, settlement, and information services to broker-dealers, banks, and mutual funds. The NSCC was established in 1976 to handle clearance and settlement for its owners, the New York Stock Exchange, American Stock Exchange, and the National Association of Securities Dealers, Inc. The NSCC is a clearing agency registered with the SEC. http://www.nscc.com

Net credit or net debit position

A participant's net credit or net debit position (in funds or in a particular security) at settlement time is called the net settlement position. These positions may be calculated bilaterally or multilaterally.

Net Settlement

A settlement in which a number of transactions between or among counterparties are settled on a net basis.

Netting

An agreement to offset mutual positions or obligations by participants in a clearance or settlement system. The netting reduces the number of individual positions. Netting may take several forms, some of which are more legally enforceable than others in the event of default of one of the parties.

Nominee

A person or entity named by another to act on his behalf. Securities are commonly held in nominee name (often the custodian's name) to facilitate their registration and changes in their legal ownership. A nominee does not have any rights of ownership.

Omgeo

A global joint venture formed by the Depository Trust & Clearing Corporation (DTCC) and Thomson Financial ESG. Omgeo's objectives are to deliver a single, global trade management solution that will help move the industry towards global STP and T+1 settlement. http://www.omgeo.com

Omnibus account

A collective account holding the securities that a custodian safeguards on behalf of some or all of its customers.

Open transactions
Transactions having no fixed maturity date.

Physical delivery
Delivery of the security as actual paper stock or bond certificate.

Physical securities
Securities that are in certificate (paper) form.

Pre-matching process
Process by which counterparties compare trade or settlement information before other matching or comparison procedures are followed. Generally, pre-matching does not bind counterparties. See confirmation/affirmation process.

Primary custodian
For purposes of the Investment Company Act of 1940, a primary custodian is a bank or qualified foreign bank that contracts directly with a mutual fund to provide custodial services related to maintaining the fund's assets outside the United States. Also called global custodian.

Prime brokerage
The provision by firms (typically large securities houses) of credit, clearing, securities lending, and other services to clients (typically hedge funds).

Principal
A party to a transaction that acts on its own behalf. In acting as a principal, a firm is buying/selling (or lending/borrowing) for its own account.

Provisional transfer
A conditional transfer in which one or more parties retain the right by law or agreement to rescind the transfer.

Qualified vendor
A vendor of electronic confirmation and affirmation services that meets the standards prescribed by NYSE Rule 387. See Appendix D.

Real-time gross settlement (RTGS)
In a **real-time system**, a transfer (of a payment or securities) will reach its destination within minutes (if not seconds) of being debited from the sending

participant's account. In a **gross settlement system**, each transfer is handled individually. In a real-time gross settlement (RTGS) system, execution of each transaction or payment order will be handled individually when received, and acknowledgement will be sent to the participants in real-time. Fedwire, CHAPs, and TARGET are examples of RTGS payment systems.

Rebate
The interest rate that a securities lender pays the borrower on cash collateral.

Recall
A demand by a securities lender that a borrower return securities lent in an open transaction.

Record date
The date on which the shareholder must officially own the security in order to be entitled to the dividend. After the record date, the security is ex-dividend. See ex-dividend.

Repurchase agreement (repo)
A contract to sell securities and subsequently to repurchase them at a specified price and typically at a specified time. Repos, which are typically executed on U.S. government securities, are usually very short term.

Reverse repurchase agreement (reverse repo)
A contract to purchase securities and subsequently to resell them at a specified date and price.

Safekeeping
A custodian's or depository's holding of physical (certificated) or immobilized securities.

Same day funds
Money balances that the recipient has a right to transfer or withdraw from an account on the day of receipt.

SAS 70
Statement of Accounting Standard No. 70, "Reports on the Processing of Transactions by Service Organizations." A SAS 70 is an examination of an organization's internal control structure; it may or may not include testing. Banks providing custody services to institutional customers typically have an

annual SAS 70 performed by an independent auditor. Statements of accounting standards are issued by the Auditing Standards Board of the Association of Independent Certified Public Accountants. [In the United Kingdom, a FRAG-21 is similar to a SAS 70.]

Securities depository
See central securities depository.

Securities Movement and Control (SMAC)
A written or computerized set of rules designed to ensure the safe movement of certificates or book-entry securities. Computerized SMAC systems are used as a control for book-entry securities and to monitor the purchases and sales of physical securities from the time a trade is executed until the securities arrive at the bank or leave it, or until the securities are transferred on the books of the depository. SMAC systems will generally contain security master files and client master files.

Securities settlement system (SSS)
A system, frequently a central securities depository, in which the settlement of securities takes place. Sometimes called a clearing system.

Stock Exchange Daily Official List (SEDOL)
Numbering system that the London Stock Exchange uses for UK securities and other securities.

Segregation
Optional or compulsory separation of a participant's own securities from those held on behalf of its customers.

Settlement
The completion of a securities transaction between participants. A trade has settled when the participants discharge their contractual obligations and exchange funds for securities.

Settlement cycle
The amount of time that elapses between the trade date (T) and the settlement date. Typically measured relative to the trade date. For example, in a T + 3 settlement cycle settlement occurs on the third business day following the trade date.

Settlement date
The date by which an executed trade order must settle or fail, or the date that the parties to a securities transaction agree that settlement is to take place. See contractual settlement.

Special (collateral)
Securities that are highly sought after in the market by borrowers.

Standard settlement instructions (SSI)
Delivery instructions established between counterparties that may be transmitted as part of an electronic trade confirmation (e.g., Society for Worldwide Interbank Financial Telecommunication) message.

Straight-Through Processing
The **ISSA** definition: "To provide an open gateway to a common and standard transaction structure that eliminates repetitive data entry, from order generation to settlement completion for all markets, instruments, and participants."

Sub-custodian
The local custodian through whom the global custodian holds securities. See local agent, local custodian.

Substitution
Recalling the securities lent from a borrower and replacing them with other securities of equivalent market value during the life of the securities loan.

The Society for Worldwide Interbank Financial Telecommunication (S.W.I.F.T.)
A bank-owned organization providing secure messaging services to thousands of banks in nearly 200 countries, **S.W.I.F.T.** is also officially designated by the International Organization for Standardization (ISO) to maintain message standards within the securities industry. http://www.swift.com

Trans-European Automated Real-time Gross Settlement Express Transfer System (TARGET)
A payment system that interlinks all of the national real-time gross settlement systems in the EU member states. TARGET is located at the European Central Bank. http://www.ecb.int

Tax Reclaims
Service provided by global custodians involving reclaiming recoverable portions of taxes withheld from interest or dividend payments by foreign taxation authorities. Tax relief is governed by tax treaties between countries.

Term transactions
Transactions with a fixed maturity date.

Trade date
The date on which a securities transaction is executed.

Tri-party repo
A repurchase agreement in which bonds and cash are delivered by the trading counterparty to an independent custodian bank, clearing house, or securities depository that is responsible for ensuring that the collateral's value remains adequate during the life of the transaction.

Unwind
A procedure followed in certain clearing and settlement systems in which transfers of securities and funds are settled on a net basis at the end of the processing cycle. All transfers are provisional until all participants have discharged their settlement obligations. If a participant fails to settle, some or all of the provisional transfers involving that participant are deleted from the system, and the settlement obligations from the remaining transfers are recalculated.

Value at Risk (VAR)
The estimate of the maximum amount that the value of covered positions could decline during a fixed holding period within a stated confidence level.

Withholding tax
A tax on income deducted at the source. A paying agent is legally obliged to deduct withholding tax from its payments of interest on deposits, securities, or similar financial instruments.

Zero hour rule
A law in some countries that allows a bankruptcy declared by a court during the day to be declared retroactive to 0.00 a.m. of the same day. This law retroactively renders invalid all transactions of the bankrupt entity that took place after 0.00 a.m. on that date.

Custody Services   Appendix B

Corporate Actions

The different types of corporate actions, and the terminology used to describe them, may vary by country and market. This list identifies some common corporate actions. Actions marked by an asterisk (*) are voluntary; such actions typically require a customer decision within a short time frame.

Bond Calls
The right to redeem outstanding bonds prior to their scheduled maturity.

Bonus Share Plan
Allows shareholders the option of receiving their cash dividend in the form of additional shares. Discounts toward the purchase of additional shares are usually offered. Similar to a dividend reinvestment plan.

* Capital Gains Distribution
Realization of capital either in shares or cash.

* Cash/Stock Option Dividend
Shareholder has the option of receiving cash dividends or additional shares. The shares are offered at a specific ratio (for example, one new share for each 50 shares owned).

Class Action
Technically not corporate action but managed in a similar manner. A class action is a court action filed on behalf of a group of shareholders. In a class action, shareholders who purchased or sold the company's securities during a specific period of time, known as the class period, usually allege that the company and its officers and directors violated federal and state securities laws.

* Convertible Securities
Corporate bonds or preferred stock that the holder can exchange, at his or her option, for another type of security (typically common stock) at a set price. The conversion ratio determines how many shares of common stock will be received in exchange for the convertible security at the time of conversion.

Dividend Option
A dividend payment that carries an option to accept stock in place of cash.

* Dividend Reinvestment Plan (DRIP)
A plan sponsored by an issuer that allows shareholders to buy the company's stock with their cash dividends.

Mergers/Takeovers
The merger of two or more companies under a single corporate structure or the acquisition of one of more companies by another company. Payments may be in the form of shares of the resulting company, cash, or a combination of the two. A name change may also be involved.

Mini-Tenders
Tender offers for less than 5 percent of a company's stock. Mini-tender offers typically do not provide the same disclosure and procedural protection that larger, traditional tender offers provide.

* Nominal Change
A change in a security's par value to its current price in the market.

* Optional Conversions
Conversions in which the customer has the option of converting a security into more than one other security (i.e., warrants, stock, bonds).

*Options and Warrants
These actions come in two forms, convertible at any time during their life, or convertible on a set date.

* Placings
Issues of new shares that are privately placed with larger institutions (or new issues for which larger institutions are given preference). Not generally offered to the public.

* Proxies
A document that enables shareholders to vote on a company's proposals without attending the shareholder meeting.

---

* Redemption

Maturity of a debt security when the nominal value becomes due and payable to the holder. Types of redemptions include maturities, calls, and sinking fund redemptions. Redemptions may be partial.

* Rights Issue

An offering allowing existing shareholders to purchase newly issued stock by means of rights which can be traded, exercised, or allowed to expire. The number of rights offered to each shareholder is calculated by inserting the shareholder's existing holding in a predetermined formula. In most cases, the price per share available to shareholders is lower than the market price.

Stock Bonus Issue

Similar to a stock dividend. The issue of stock to existing shareholders at a set ratio.

Stock Dividend

Dividend paid in additional shares of stock. In certain countries these issues may be traded for a short period of time.

Stockholder Meeting Announcements

Announcements of regularly scheduled and special stockholder meetings. Meeting announcements and any accompanying proxy materials are typically passed on to the beneficial owners of the securities.

Stock Split/Par Value Change

Issuance of additional stock to existing shareholders, typically expressed as a ratio (e.g., 2-for-1 split). In a reverse split, the number of shares are reduced (e.g., a 1-for-3 ratio of new shares for old).

Subdivision

The division of existing stock into a greater number of shares of lesser value; the overall value of the holdings is unchanged. Similar to a stock split.

Subscription

An issuance of stock in which preference is given to existing shareholders. An existing stockholder is allowed to purchase the new shares before the public can, typically at a discounted price.

*Tender Offer

A formal offer to purchase a holder's shares at a price higher than the market price. The offer may be for all of the outstanding shares or just a portion.

Custody Services   Appendix C

Investment Company Act of 1940

15 U.S.C. 80a-17(f) — Investment Company Act of 1940
17 CFR 270.17f — Rules and Regulation, Investment Company Act of 1940

Rule17f-4 Deposits of securities in securities depositories.

(a) For the purpose of this rule, a "securities depository" is a system for the central handling of securities where all securities of any particular class or series of any issuer deposited within the system are treated as fungible and may be transferred or pledged by bookkeeping entry without physical delivery of the securities.

(b) A registered management investment company (investment company) or any qualified custodian may deposit all or any part of the securities owned by the investment company in an Eligible Securities Depository as defined in Sec. 270.17f-7 in accordance with the provisions of Sec. 270.17f-7 and applicable provisions of Sec. 270.17f-5, or in:
   (1) A clearing agency registered with the Commission under section 17A of the Securities Exchange Act of 1934 (clearing agency), which acts as a securities depository, or
   (2) The book-entry system as provided in subpart O of Treasury Circular No. 300, 31 CFR part 306, subpart B of 31 CFR part 350, and the book-entry regulations of Federal agencies substantially in the form of subpart O, in accordance with the following paragraphs of this section.

(c) An investment company may deposit the securities in a clearing agency which acts as a securities depository under an arrangement that contains the following elements:
   (1) The investment company has a system that is reasonably designed to prevent unauthorized officer's instructions and which provides, at least, for the form, content, and means of giving, recording, and reviewing the instructions. An "officer's instruction" is a request or direction to a clearing agency in the name of the investment company by one or more persons authorized by its board of directors to give it.

(2) Upon ceasing to act for an investment company, and subject to its own rules on contributions to a participants fund, the clearing agency shall deliver all securities held for the investment company to a successor clearing agency, custodian, or safekeeper under Rule 17f-2 (17 CFR 270.17f-2), to be named by the investment company. Where the investment company has not named one, the clearing agency shall deliver the investment company securities to a bank having the qualifications prescribed in section 26(a)(1) of the Act for trustees of unit investment trusts, to be held by the bank as custodian for the investment company under terms customary to a custodian agreement between banks and investment companies.

(3) The investment company, by resolution of its board of directors, initially approved the arrangement, and any subsequent changes thereto.

(d) The custodian may deposit the securities in a clearing agency which acts as a securities depository or the book-entry system, or both, under an arrangement that contains the following elements:

(1) The custodian may deposit the securities directly or through one or more agents which are also qualified to act as custodians for investment companies.

(2) The custodian (or its agent) shall deposit the securities in an account that includes only assets held by it for customers.

(3) The custodian shall send the investment company a confirmation of any transfers to or from the account of the investment company. Where securities are transferred to that account, the custodian shall also, by book-entry or otherwise, identify as belonging to the investment company a quantity of securities in a fungible bulk of securities (i) registered in the name of the custodian (or its nominee) or (ii) shown on the custodian's account on the books of the clearing agency, the book-entry system, or the custodian's agent. for this purpose, the term "confirmation" means advice or notice of a transaction; it is not intended to require preparation by a custodian of the confirmation required of broker-dealers under the Securities Exchange Act of 1934.

(4) The custodian, or its agent which deposits the securities, shall promptly send to the investment company reports it receives from the appropriate Federal Reserve Bank or clearing agency on its respective system of internal accounting control. The custodian and all the agents through which the securities are deposited shall send to the investment company such reports on their own systems of internal accounting control as the investment company may reasonably request from time to time.

(5) The investment company, by resolution of its board of directors,

initially approved the arrangement, and any subsequent changes thereto.

Rule 17f-5 Custody of investment company assets outside the United States.

(a) Definitions. For purposes of this section:

(1) Eligible Foreign Custodian means an entity that is incorporated or organized under the laws of a country other than the United States and that is a Qualified Foreign Bank or a majority-owned direct or indirect subsidiary of a U.S. Bank or bank-holding company.

(2) Foreign Assets means any investments (including foreign currencies) for which the primary market is outside the United States, and any cash and cash equivalents that are reasonably necessary to effect the Fund's transactions in those investments.

(3) Foreign Custody Manager means a Fund's or a Registered Canadian Fund's board of directors or any person serving as the board's delegate under paragraphs (b) or (d) of this section.

(4) Fund means a management investment company registered under the Act (15 U.S.C. 80a) and incorporated or organized under the laws of the United States or of a state.

(5) Qualified Foreign Bank means a banking institution or trust company, incorporated or organized under the laws of a country other than the United States, that is regulated as such by the country's government or an agency of the country's government.

(6) Registered Canadian Fund means a management investment company incorporated or organized under the laws of Canada and registered under the Act pursuant to the conditions of Sec. 270.7d-1.

(7) U.S. Bank means an entity that is:

(i) A banking institution organized under the laws of the United States;

(ii) A member bank of the Federal Reserve System;

(iii) Any other banking institution or trust company organized under the laws of any state or of the United States, whether incorporated or not, doing business under the laws of any state or of the United States, a substantial portion of the business of which consists of receiving deposits or exercising fiduciary powers similar to those permitted to national banks under the authority of the Comptroller of the Currency, and which is supervised and examined by state or federal authority having supervision over banks, and which is not operated for the purpose of evading the provisions of this section; or

(iv) A receiver, conservator, or other liquidating agent of any institution or firm included in paragraphs (a)(7)(i), (ii), or (iii) of this section.

(b) Delegation. A Fund's board of directors may delegate to the fund's investment adviser or officers or to a U.S. Bank or to a Qualified Foreign Bank the responsibilities set forth in paragraphs (c)(1), (c)(2), or (c)(3) of this section, provided that:

(1) Reasonable Reliance. The board determines that it is reasonable to rely on the delegate to perform the delegated responsibilities;

(2) Reporting. The board requires the delegate to provide written reports notifying the board of the placement of Foreign Assets with a particular custodian and of any material change in the Fund's foreign custody arrangements, with the reports to be provided to the board at such times as the board deems reasonable and appropriate based on the circumstances of the Fund's arrangements; and

(3) Exercise of Care. The delegate agrees to exercise reasonable care, prudence and diligence such as a person having responsibility for the safekeeping of the Fund's Foreign Assets would exercise, or to adhere to a higher standard of care, in performing the delegated responsibilities.

(c) Maintaining Assets with an Eligible Foreign Custodian. A Fund or its Foreign Custody Manager may place and maintain the Fund's Foreign Assets in the care of an Eligible Foreign Custodian, provided that:

(1) General Standard. The Foreign Custody Manager determines that the Foreign Assets will be subject to reasonable care, based on the standards applicable to custodians in the relevant market, if maintained with the Eligible Foreign Custodian, after considering all factors relevant to the safekeeping of the Foreign Assets, including, without limitation:

(i) The Eligible Foreign Custodian's practices, procedures, and internal controls, including, but not limited to, the physical protections available for certificated securities (if applicable), the method of keeping custodial records, and the security and data protection practices;

(ii) Whether the Eligible Foreign Custodian has the requisite financial strength to provide reasonable care for Foreign Assets;

(iii) The Eligible Foreign Custodian's general reputation and standing; and

(iv) Whether the Fund will have jurisdiction over and be able to enforce judgments against the Eligible Foreign Custodian, such as by virtue of the existence of offices in the United States or consent to service of process in the United States.

(2) Contract. The arrangement with the Eligible Foreign Custodian is governed by a written contract that the Foreign Custody Manager has

determined will provide reasonable care for Foreign Assets based on the standards specified in paragraph (c)(1) of this section.

(i) The contract must provide:

(A) For indemnification or insurance arrangements (or any combination) that will adequately protect the Fund against the risk of loss of Foreign Assets held in accordance with the contract;

(B) That the Foreign Assets will not be subject to any right, charge, security interest, lien or claim of any kind in favor of the Eligible Foreign Custodian or its creditors, except a claim of payment for their safe custody or administration or, in the case of cash deposits, liens or rights in favor of creditors of the custodian arising under bankruptcy, insolvency, or similar laws;

(C) That beneficial ownership of the Foreign Assets will be freely transferable without the payment of money or value other than for safe custody or administration;

(D) That adequate records will be maintained identifying the Foreign Assets as belonging to the Fund or as being held by a third party for the benefit of the Fund;

(E) That the Fund's independent public accountants will be given access to those records or confirmation of the contents of those records; and

(F) That the Fund will receive periodic reports with respect to the safekeeping of the Foreign Assets, including, but not limited to, notification of any transfer to or from the Fund's account or a third-party account containing assets held for the benefit of the Fund.

(ii) The contract may contain, in lieu of any or all of the provisions specified in paragraph (c)(2)(i) of this section, other provisions that the Foreign Custody Manager determines will provide, in their entirety, the same or a greater level of care and protection for the Foreign Assets as the specified provisions, in their entirety.

(3)(i) Monitoring the Foreign Custody Arrangements. The Foreign Custody Manager has established a system to monitor the appropriateness of maintaining the Foreign Assets with a particular custodian under paragraph (c)(1) of this section, and to monitor performance of the contract under paragraph (c)(2) of this section.

(ii) If an arrangement with an Eligible Foreign Custodian no longer meets the requirements of this section, the Fund must withdraw the Foreign Assets from the Eligible Foreign Custodian as soon as reasonably practicable.

(d) Registered Canadian Funds. Any Registered Canadian Fund may place and maintain its Foreign Assets outside the United States in accordance with the requirements of this section, provided that:

(1) The Foreign Assets are placed in the care of an overseas branch of a U.S. Bank that has aggregate capital, surplus, and undivided profits of a specified amount, which must not be less than $500,000; and

(2) The Foreign Custody Manager is the Fund's board of directors, its investment adviser or officers, or a U.S. Bank.

Note to Sec. 270.17f-5: When a Fund's (or its custodian's) custody arrangement with an Eligible Securities Depository (as defined in Sec. 270.17f-7) involves one or more Eligible Foreign Custodians through which assets are maintained with the Eligible Securities Depository, Sec. 270.17f-5 will govern the Fund's (or its custodian's) use of each Eligible Foreign Custodian, while Sec. 270.17f-7 will govern an Eligible Foreign Custodian's use of the Eligible Securities Depository.

Rule 17f-7 Custody of investment company assets with a foreign securities depository.

(a) Custody arrangement with an eligible securities depository. A Fund, including a Registered Canadian Fund, may place and maintain its Foreign Assets with an Eligible Securities Depository, provided that:

(1) Risk-limiting safeguards. The custody arrangement provides reasonable safeguards against the custody risks associated with maintaining assets with the Eligible Securities Depository, including:

(i) Risk analysis and monitoring. (A) The fund or its investment adviser has received from the Primary Custodian (or its agent) an analysis of the custody risks associated with maintaining assets with the Eligible Securities Depository; and

(B) The contract between the Fund and the Primary Custodian requires the Primary Custodian (or its agent) to monitor the custody risks associated with maintaining assets with the Eligible Securities Depository on a continuing basis, and promptly notify the Fund or its investment adviser of any material change in these risks.

(ii) Exercise of care. The contract between the Fund and the Primary Custodian states that the Primary Custodian will agree to exercise reasonable care, prudence, and diligence in performing the requirements of paragraphs (a)(1)(i)(A) and (B) of this section, or adhere to a higher standard of care.

(2) Withdrawal of assets from eligible securities depository. If a custody arrangement with an Eligible Securities Depository no longer meets the

requirements of this section, the Fund's Foreign Assets must be withdrawn from the depository as soon as reasonably practicable.

(b) Definitions. The terms Foreign Assets, Fund, Qualified Foreign Bank, Registered Canadian Fund, and U.S. Bank have the same meanings as in Sec. 270.17f-5. In addition:

(1) Eligible Securities Depository means a system for the central handling of securities as defined in Sec. 270.17f-4 that:

(i) Acts as or operates a system for the central handling of securities or equivalent book-entries in the country where it is incorporated, or a transnational system for the central handling of securities or equivalent book-entries;

(ii) Is regulated by a foreign financial regulatory authority as defined under section 2(a)(50) of the Act (15 U.S.C. 80a-2(a)(50));

(iii) Holds assets for the custodian that participates in the system on behalf of the Fund under safekeeping conditions no less favorable than the conditions that apply to other participants;

(iv) Maintains records that identify the assets of each participant and segregate the system's own assets from the assets of participants;

(v) Provides periodic reports to its participants with respect to its safekeeping of assets, including notices of transfers to or from any participant's account; and

(vi) Is subject to periodic examination by regulatory authorities or independent accountants.

(2) Primary Custodian means a U.S. Bank or Qualified Foreign Bank that contracts directly with a Fund to provide custodial services related to maintaining the Fund's assets outside the United States.

Note to Sec. 270.17f-7: When a Fund's (or its custodian's) custody arrangement with an Eligible Securities Depository involves one or more Eligible Foreign Custodians (as defined in Sec. 270.17f-5) through which assets are maintained with the Eligible Securities Depository, Sec. 270.17f-5 will govern the Fund's (or its custodian's) use of each Eligible Foreign Custodian, while Sec. 270.17f-7 will govern an Eligible Foreign Custodian's use of the Eligible Securities Depository.

Custody Services   Appendix D

New York Stock Exchange Rule 387

(a) No member organization shall accept an order from a customer pursuant to an arrangement whereby payment for securities purchased or delivery of securities sold is to be made to or by an agent of the customer unless all of the following procedures are followed:

(1) The member or member organization shall have received from the customer prior to or at the time of accepting the order, the name and address of the agent and the name and account number of the customer on file with the agent.

(2) Each order accepted from the customer pursuant to such an arrangement has noted thereon the fact that it is a payment on delivery (POD) or collect on delivery (COD) transaction.

(3) The member organization delivers to the customer a confirmation, or all relevant data customarily contained in a confirmation with respect to the execution of the order, in whole or in part, not later than the close of business on the next business day after any such execution, and

(4) The member organization has obtained an agreement from the customer that the customer will furnish his agent instructions with respect to the receipt or delivery of the securities involved in the transaction promptly upon receipt by the customer of each confirmation, or the relevant data as to each execution, relating to such order (even though such execution represents the purchase or sale of only a part of the order), and that in any event the customer will assure that such instructions are delivered to his agent no later than:

  i) in the case of a purchase by the customer where the agent is to receive the securities against payment (COD), the close of business on the second business day after the date of execution of the trade as to which the particular confirmation relates; or

  (ii) in the case of a sale by the customer where the agent is to deliver the securities against payment (POD), the close of business on the first business day after the date of execution of the trade as to which the particular confirmation relates.

(5) The facilities of a Clearing Agency shall be utilized for the book-entry settlement of all depository eligible transactions. The facilities of either a Clearing Agency or a Qualified Vendor shall be utilized for the electronic confirmation and affirmation of all depository eligible transactions.

Supplemental Material:

.10 Transactions that are to be settled outside of the United States shall be exempt from the provisions of paragraph (a)(5) of this Rule.

.30 For purposes of this rule, a "Clearing Agency" shall mean a Clearing Agency as defined in Section 3(a)(23) of the Securities Exchange Act of 1934, that is registered with the Securities and Exchange Commission ("Commission") pursuant to Section 17A(b)(2) of the Act or has obtained from the Commission an exemption from registration granted specifically to allow the Clearing Agency to provide confirmation and affirmation services.

.40 For purposes of this rule, "depository eligible transactions" shall mean transactions in those securities for which confirmation, affirmation, and book entry settlement can be performed through the facilities of a Clearing Agency as defined in Rule 387.30.

.50 "Qualified Vendor" shall mean a vendor of electronic confirmation and affirmation services that:

(A) shall, for each transaction subject to this rule: (i) deliver a trade record to a Clearing Agency in the Clearing Agency's format; (ii) obtain a control number for the trade record from the Clearing Agency; (iii) cross-reference the control number to the confirmation and subsequent affirmation of the trade; and (iv) include the control number when delivering the affirmation of the trade to the Clearing Agency;

(B) certifies to its customers that (i) with respect to its electronic trade confirmation/affirmation system, that it has a capacity requirements, evaluation, and monitoring process that allows the vendor to formulate current and anticipated estimated capacity requirements; (ii) that its electronic trade confirmation/affirmation system has sufficient capacity to process the specified volume of data that it reasonably anticipates to be entered into its electronic trade confirmation/affirmation service during the upcoming year; (iii) that its electronic trade confirmation/affirmation system has formal contingency procedures, that the entity has followed a formal process of reviewing the likelihood of contingency occurrences, and that the contingency protocols are reviewed and updated on a regular basis; (iv) that its electronic trade confirmation/affirmation system has a process for preventing, detecting, and controlling any potential or actual systems integrity failures, and its procedures designed to protect against security breaches are followed; and (v) that its current assets exceed its current liabilities by at least five hundred thousand dollars;

(C) has submitted and shall continue to submit on an annual basis, an Auditor's Report to the Commission staff which is not deemed unacceptable by the Commission. An Auditor's Report will be deemed unacceptable if it contains any findings of material weakness;

(D) notifies the Commission staff immediately in writing of any changes to its systems that significantly affect or have the potential to significantly affect its electronic trade confirmation/affirmation systems including, without limitation, changes that: (i) affect or potentially affect the capacity or security of its electronic trade confirmation/affirmation system; (ii) rely on new or substantially different technology; or (iii) provide a new service to the Qualified Vendor's electronic trade confirmation/affirmation system;

(E) immediately notifies the Commission staff in writing if it intends to cease providing services;

(F) provides the Exchange with copies of any submissions to the Commission staff made pursuant to .50 (B), (C), (D) and (E) of this rule within ten business days; and

(G) supplies supplemental information regarding their electronic trade confirmation/affirmation services as requested by the Exchange or the Commission staff.

.60 "Auditor's Report" shall mean a written report which is prepared by competent, independent, external audit personnel in accordance with the standards of the American Institute of Certified Public Accountants and the

Information Systems Audit and Control Association and which (i) verifies the certifications contained in .50(B) above; (ii) contains a risk analysis of all aspects of the entity's information technology systems including, without limitation, computer operations, telecommunications, data security, systems development, capacity planning and testing, and contingency planning and testing; and (iii) contains the written response of the entity's management to the information provided pursuant to (i) and (ii) above.

As of May 17, 2012, this guidance applies to federal savings associations in addition to national banks.*

Custody Services   References

Laws

15 USC 80a-17(f), Investment Company Act of 1940

29 USC 1001, Employee Retirement Income Security Act of 1974

31 USC 5311-5330, Bank Secrecy Act

Regulations

12 CFR 21.21, Bank Secrecy Act Compliance

12 CFR 204, Regulation D

12 CFR 221, Regulation U

17 CFR 270.17f, Rules and Regulation, Investment Company Act of 1940

31 CFR 103, Financial Recordkeeping and Reporting of Currency and Foreign Transactions

Comptroller's Handbook Booklets

"Asset Management"

"Asset Securitization"

"Bank Secrecy Act/Anti-Money Laundering"

"Community Bank Fiduciary Activities Supervision"

"Internal and External Audits"

"Internal Control"

"Large Bank Supervision"

"Management Information Systems"

"Mortgage Banking"

"Risk Management of Financial Derivatives"

OCC Issuances

Banking Circular 196, "Securities Lending FFIEC Statement" (Revised)

Banking Circular 275, "Free Riding in Custody Accounts"

Other

Department of Labor Advisory Opinions
    97-15A (Frost Letter)
    97-16A (Aetna Letter)
Department of Labor Prohibited Transaction Exemptions
    81-6 (January 23, 1981)
    82-63 (April 6, 1982)
    84-14 (March 13, 1984)
    96-23 (April 10, 1996)
    98-54 (November 13, 1998)
FFIEC Information Systems Handbook
Group of 30 Recommendations (1989)
New York Stock Exchange Rule 387
Harris Trust v. Salomon Smith Barney, 530 U.S. 238 (2000)